Going to Church to Catch HELL

Kermeshea Hilliard Evans

Job 2 [10]
But Job replied, ".... Should we accept only good things from the hand of God and never anything bad?" ... (New Living Translation)

Going to Church to Catch HELL

Kermeshea Hilliard Evans

New Era 4 Life Publishing

HOUSTON

NEW ERA 4 LIFE PUBLISHING EDITION, JUNE 2010

COPYRIGHT ©2010 BY KERMESHEA EVANS

ALL RIGHTS RESERVED UNDER INTERNATIONAL AND PAN-AMERICAN COPYRIGHT CONVENTIONS. PUBLISHED IN THE UNITED STATES BY NEW ERA FOR LIFE PUBLISHING.

ALL REFERENCES TO THE BIBLE ARE FROM THE KING JAMES VERSION, UNLESS OTHERWISE NOTED.

ISBN 9-78-14536-5916-8

ARTISTIC DESIGN BY
ROCSTAR MILES

PRINTED IN THE UNITED STATES OF AMERICA

WWW.KERMESHEAEVANS.NING.COM
WWW.FACEBOOK.COM/GOINGTOCHURCHTOCATCHHELL
ROCSTARMILES@GMAIL.COM

This book is dedicated to Simuel, my husband, who has taught and shown me unconditional love, a lesson that I should have learned much earlier in life and to my children Simuel, Khristian and Stefan.

Acknowledgments

Thanks to God for His Grace, His Mercy, His Healing Touch. Thank You Lord for my second chance and for entrusting me with this life that You have given me. I am in awe of where You have brought me from and how You have carried me through. I am in eager expectation of where You are taking me. I Love You! *Among the gods there is none like unto thee, O Lord; neither are there any works like unto thy works.* (Psalm 86:8)

Thanks to my husband, Simuel who encouraged me even when I did not have the strength to listen. You are my best friend. You are my rock. You have loved me even when I did not love myself. I could not ask for a better partner in life and love. We have been through a lot and your love for me has remained the same. It's our time to make it happen. Let's get it!

To my three sons, Simuel, Khristian and Stefan. You guys are all so handsome and intelligent with a great sense of humor; and just so you know you got all of those qualities from your mother. Thank you so much for being who you are to me individually. When you would walk into the room wherever I was working on this book, just to check on me or say, "Mama you are doing good," it would always make me smile knowing that I have three guys who are always in my corner. I love you Simi! I love you Khristian! I love you Stefan!

To my girl Keshia, how can I say, "Thank You" enough. You are my sister friend. Thanks for listening. Thank you for challenging me. Thanks for the encouragement. Thanks for the final two scriptures in the book. "That Will Preach Girl!"

Thank You to all of my Facebook Friends, you have encouraged me through this process without even knowing it, without a touch and without sound. Thanks for the typed words, the comments and the "likes."

To the Evans and Miles family, especially my mother-in-law, Jacqueline Evans and my grandmother-in-law, Pauline Miles, your love has seen me through. There is no better hug in the world than a Ma-Dear hug! My brother-in-laws, Cedric and Josh, my sister-in-laws, Cassandra and Jackie, my niece and nephews... I love you all!

Thank you to a man of God, who I have adopted as my "virtual Pastor." Thank you for caring enough to share your wisdom. There is no replacement for wise counsel.

Lastly, to the Body of Christ, Thank you for your prayers. I do not know who was praying for me but I know that you were lifting me up and interceding on my behalf. I am forever grateful.

Love,

Kermeshea

GOING TO CHURCH TO CATCH HELL

Isaiah 49 [15]

Can a woman forget her nursing child? Will she have no compassion on the child from her womb? Although mothers may forget,   I will not forget you.

(God's Word Translation)

My Mother

For as long as I can remember, I have known that I was an unwanted child. That's not so much of a big deal, I recognize that there are abandoned children who never know their birth parents. There are children who hear their parents say, "We did not plan to have you" or "You definitely were a surprise." My situation is a little different. By different, I do not mean better or worse, my situation was just what it was...unlike most.

When I was 18 months old, my mother remarried. The courtship was just a few months. A small wedding on a Saturday and on Sunday, my new father was confirmed as the Pastor of his first church. We were Baptists. For me, this meant that I spent my childhood in church. I was there three times Sunday, Monday night, Wednesday night, Thursday night and most Saturday mornings. I survived my first church fight around age six; the members planned to harm my sister and I with poisoned candy.

Eventually, my father would leave the Baptist church, start his own independent church and claim his spot in the new movement of Word of Faith churches. Not long after the transition from Baptist to Word of Faith, my mother joined him in the pulpit, ministering to what would soon become masses.

They were both great story tellers, captivating even. My mother was passionate in her delivery, my father's delivery was simplistic and eye opening. They both prided themselves on being transparent from the pulpit and using their own life experience's to provide modern examples of Biblical principles. I learned very early on that the church was the family business and my parent's "open book" approach did not just include their lives, it encompassed mine as well.

I recall sitting in church on Sunday and out of nowhere my mother would relive the mistakes of her past attempting to inspire the crowd. Somehow, I would always be the central part of her speech. My mother's story of her mistake as it related to me was not unique; in fact, it's been told a thousand times over.

Even if you never heard my mother tell it, you have no doubt heard the story. Naive girl goes to her high school prom, loses her virginity to the boy she thought would love her forever and nine months later she births a baby that her conscious, or worse, her parents would not allow her to abort or place for adoption. When my mother told her story, she was always the victim, my new father was her godsend and I was just the visible proof of her prom night mistake relived. No matter where I sat in the congregation as she told her story, I could not escape the stares. I had three sisters and even without my mother mentioning my name, it seemed that everyone always knew that the shame my mother spoke of was me. If I were seated in the back people would turn and gawk, if I were seated in the front, I would feel the heat of what seemed like a million laser eyes on my back.

I often wondered does she hate me that much, that she would embarrass me without regard. So, one day when I was around 12, after sitting through my mother tell of her mistake at a women's conference, I finally gathered enough courage to approach my mother about the message of her mistake and how it made me feel. I explained to her that every time she told the story, it made me feel as if she did not like me and as eloquently as I could articulate my feelings at that age, I told my mother, "I just don't like it when you do that." My mother, listened and acknowledged that she hadn't considered my feelings. She made her best attempt to confirm for me that she always loved me and always will.

Later that night, my mother returned to the stage at the same conference and surprised me by openly apologizing to me for referring to me as a mistake. I remember feeling as if my mother had finally given me her stamp of approval. For that moment, I thought all was good. It was short lived. One would think that after the apology there would be no more mention of the prom night mistake. Of course, the story still had to be told so instead of a mistake, I became her testimony.

From that moment forward, I developed "tough skin." I became emotionless. I did not cry, my new father said it was a sign of weakness. To "make me ready" for a life of ministry, my father would remind me daily that God had put me in the family because He knew that I could handle the persecution that comes with being a part of the First Family. My life, all twelve years of it, had to be shared to bless others. Sadly, I bought into that, believed and lived it for too long; years that I cannot get back. I abandoned all attempts to articulate my feelings, good, bad or indifferent. I internalized my emotions and cultivated a guarded persona that did not encompass who God intended me to be.

As an adult, I understand that my mother needed an outlet to voice her pain. She did not have a support group or any other venue to talk through her pain. Seeking out a therapist or counseling from a spiritual advisor would destroy the "we are in complete control" image that she and my father had worked so desperately to achieve.

I can only imagine that every time my mother looked at me, she saw a piece of the man who had taken her innocence and left her to deal with the guilt of not knowing better and the disgrace of teenage pregnancy. As a child should I have been subjected to carrying the hurt of my mother's pain? I now know that hurt people tend to hurt others, whether unintentionally or on purpose.

Years passed and at age twenty-six my mother's pain would not allow her to love me unconditionally through a difficult period of my life. My mother's final words to me were in a letter delivered in a brown envelope through Regular First Class Mail. The value of my mother's first born child had diminished to that of a 32 cents stamp. Her words in the letter were perhaps a final release of all the pain that I had inadvertently caused her just by being born. She wrote, "Your father and I have made the decision to disinherit you, we have legally removed you from all of our final wills, you are no longer a part of us... As a family, we have decided you do not exist." The entire family had decided to live out a lie with no regard for others.

Was I shocked? Not really. In a way, I knew that my mother would choose consequence over truth. At that moment, physically I felt relieved. It was as if a boulder sized burden had been lifted. Admittedly, it hurt and it would take almost a decade before I found the strength to allow my hurt to heal.

It still amazes me that when my mother decided that I no longer existed, my portion of her testimony faded from her memory. I guess the unwanted child was no longer a mistake from her past or a part of her life testimony. My mother who ministered to others about faith confessions, believing God and never giving up on your children, had made herself an exception to her teachings.

I learned a valuable lesson from my mother. Emotional pain is real and it hurts not only the victim but everyone around them. I have come to realize that my mother's pain is hers to own and not mine to bear. I know that God did not make a mistake the days that I was conceived or born, regardless of the circumstances surrounding my grand entrance into the world.

My Biological Father

My biological father died, May 28, 1982. I think that he was murdered in his own home. I don't really know because no one ever bothered to tell me what happened. His funeral was on a sunny day, my memory is of a small, crowded, hot white church building. My mother drove, we were late, my aunt walked me into the church. I was eight years old, standing in a packed church, holding my aunt's hand in front of a casket where my daddy lay dead. At that age, I knew enough about death to know that I would never see my daddy again. What I did not know was how I was supposed to feel about that.

The funeral is just a blurred memory for me, a lot of crying and screaming.

My biological father was a military man; United States Marine Corps, a Vietnam Veteran. His burial is very clear in my memory. Since he was not married, and I was his oldest child, I was the recipient of the flag that was a part of his burial ceremony with full military honors. My aunt stood beside me as the twenty-one gun salute went off and the flag that draped my daddy's casket was perfectly folded and handed to me by a somber, yet gracious member of the United States Military. The flag would be my only tangible memory of my biological father and that day would be the last time that I saw it. It would also be the last memory that I have of seeing any member of my daddy's family.

My Father

My father was by far the most important person in my life. Like most little girls I thought that there was nothing and no one greater than him. I never struggled with being bitter or not liking him because he was not my biological father, most likely because he was a part of my life from such a young age.

Since he had been preaching since he was a boy, he was very articulate, charismatic and quite charming. He was tall, dark and handsome. Back in the day, all the women thought he looked like Eddie Murphy, with sideburns of course. He was the type of man that commanded presence when he walked in the room. Always sharp, always looked like a man with a plan.

When my mother married my new father, I gained an older sister. She would come over to visit once or twice a month on the weekends. Eventually, when I was about seven, those visits stopped and I would not see her again until I was fourteen years old.

In the beginning, I was the only child in the house, my younger sister came along when I was 3. So my new father and I spent a great deal of time together. When he practiced his sermons for the upcoming Sunday, I was right there in the mirror next to him. If you grew up in a black Baptist church, you will understand my next statement. My hooping skills were on point, I practiced almost as much as my father did and I was good.

When I was 11, my father informed me that he would be legally adopting me. My mother explained how the process would work. A social worker was coming to visit, I needed to tell her that I enjoyed my life. I should be honest, but I did not need to tell the social worker everything. My name was going to change, I could keep my first name. My middle name would change to be the same as my mother and my granny. My last name would now be the same as my new father's.

The adoption was fine with me, I had no real memory of my biological father. I had no photos or memorabilia of him in my possession. My mother told me years earlier, that my biological father's family did not want to have any association with me. My new father was the only daddy that I knew. The adoption would make me official.

My father and I shared a special bond. He rarely called me Kermeshea. My granny had nicknamed me "poompie" when I was born, he shortened that nickname and always called me "poom." It did not matter to him where we were, if he wanted my attention he would call for "poom." As an adult, he still called me "poom," he was the only one who did, he was the only one who could.

My father could comb my hair when I was a little girl, he was not as good as my mother, but it was good enough to go out in public. As a teenager, he would be the one to sit by my bed and comfort me after my first argument with a boyfriend.

The life lessons that most of my female friends learned from their mother's, I learned from my father. He taught me how a woman should act. Before the best selling book, my father had equipped me with the skills to "act like a lady and think like a man." I remember one day, my boyfriend came over and I answered the door with curlers in my hair. When my boyfriend left, my father let me have it. He said, "That boy doesn't want to see you looking like that, you never entertain a man not looking the way you did when he met you."

My father taught me to handle criticism without crying. He made sure that I was tough. I was very much a girl, often referred to as "high maintenance" but he made certain that I was mentally strong. He taught to me to control my emotions, "no crying it makes people think you are weak," he would say. He taught me how to discern character in others "be friendly to others, but trusting of no one" he would tell me, "if you ask the right questions, you will learn all that you need to know." He would always say, "In God we trust, everyone else we check out thoroughly."

My father taught me planning and preparation. As a child, whenever I asked him for anything, I needed to be able to respond to all his questions before receiving an affirmative answer. He would ask me a series of questions, "Why do you need that?" "How much does it cost?" "What are you going to do with it when you get it?" "How is it going to help to grow as a person?" Over time, I would learn to prepare myself to answer the questions before approaching him. Sometimes he would add questions that he had not asked before. So for me to get what I wanted, I had to learn to anticipate the obstacles that he would throw my way.

My father is a reader, he enjoys it, I don't think he ever met a book that he did not like. Seeing him dedicate himself to reading, made me want to read. In our home, there was a complete wall of books, hundreds of them. Whatever my father read, I read it too. My vocabulary was extensive, I read so that I could talk to him about the books that he and I read. Reading with him expanded my world and our relationship.

Growing up, no matter how many times I saw my father throughout the day, he always made a point to kiss me on the forehead, give me a hug and tell me that he loved me. As a teenager, when I would remind him that we have already been through the I love you routine today.

My father would say, "I know but I do not ever want you to feel like you need to seek out love from a man. I don't want you to make any mistakes looking for love. So, you need to know that I love you."

I was in awe of my father. When he spoke I listened, I observed his interactions with others, his mannerisms, he was my example. To me, he always had the most accurate printed handwriting. I would do my very best to replicate it, if he left written notes laying around, I traced over the letters so that I could learn to write like him. The practice would serve me well, years later when I started to work for the church. I could always read his notes on documents and understand exactly what was written. What looked like a doctor's scribble scratch in the margins to others was perfectly legible to me.

As loving as my father was, he was also a strict disciplinarian. He did not play around when it came to following his rules. Like all my friends, I had a curfew, a time that I needed to be in the house. Unlike my friends, I had a time that I needed to be off the phone.

My sister's and I had our own phone line; my father had access to the phone line from his bedroom. If the phone rang after curfew, he would answer the phone in his bedroom. If we were on the phone after curfew he would pick up the phone and remind us that it was time to get off.

I was afraid of my father's discipline. I did not violate his rules, I did not want to be in trouble with him. I love my father. I wanted to please him, I wanted him to be proud of me. He would tell my sisters and I, if he was not around, he would still know if we did something wrong. How? God would tell him. I reverenced the wrath of God, I feared the wrath of my father.

I always viewed my father as a man of God. A dynamic minister. I regularly thought that he had a hotline to God's ear. My father the preacher and my father the man were two completely different personalities. My father the preacher is caring, confident, inspiring, uplifting. He is articulate, passionate, simplistic in style and at times comedic. My father the man is demanding, difficult and quick to judge. He is tyrannical, manipulative, cunning, controlling and critical of others. He is defensive of his own integrity and quick to attempt to discredit the integrity of others. My father has been blessed with the "gift of gab," he knows how to use words to affect others. His words are premeditated and convincing. His words are also condemning, calculating and sometimes cruel. My father the man is boastful, prideful and at times arrogant. There is a part of my father that is a jealous man, he does not like for anyone to "take his shine." As a child, it was confusing, as an adult it would leave me conflicted.

My father's personality flaws and shortcomings never redefined his level of importance in my life. I always considered him to be my ultimate authority. I allowed my father to define who I was and derived my self worth from his approval. So later in my life when my father washed his hands and threw me away like trash. I was devastated. I was crushed. I could not handle it.

A New Beginning

My early memories of church are troubling. I saw Christian people in the church act out in ways that surpassed the scandal in the world. When I was 6 or 7 years old, my father was the Senior Pastor of a Baptist Church. It was said that the members of the church had hired, tormented and fired several young Pastors before him. Knowing this, my father still accepted the job. The members of the church decided that they wanted to put my father out, but he was not leaving. The result, a colossal church fight.

The elders, deacons and trustees of the church decided that if he would not willingly leave, they would force him out. As an intimidation tactic Christian people in the church brought guns to church and would display the guns like gangsters in movies. My parents had an informant in the church who would brief them on the plan of attack for the upcoming Sunday service. The members planned various hellacious activities to force our family out of the church. They planned to poison my younger sister and I by giving us tainted candy. When my mother heard this, she monitored our interactions with other people at church and warned us not to take anything from anyone. My sister and I eventually stopped attending church on Sunday with my parents, instead we went to church with my grandparents.

The elders in the church accused my father of stealing an offering tray. Not the offering in the tray, just the gold plated offering tray. My father was arrested in the pulpit on a Sunday morning and the theft of the tray was one of many trumped up charges. I watched my father as he dealt with the circumstances surrounding his arrest. He never spoke against the church or God's people. He believed that if anyone presumed his guilt,

God would rewrite his reputation in their hearts and minds.

After the arrest, my father said that God told him never to go back into that church, so he did not. He was cleared of all charges and began the process of starting over. The experience was so traumatizing for me, that I was left very bitter, I was mean to everyone. At age seven, Christian people in the church had displayed characteristics so foul that it altered the dynamic of my youthful innocence and damaged my ability to trust. When my mother received the message on faith and the power of words, she wrote a confession specifically for me so that I could be healed of the distress from the church fight. The confession was that God would erase the pain of the situation from my heart, that I would treat others as Christ would have me to and when I speak, the compassion of Jesus flows from my mouth. The confession was pasted to the mirror in my bathroom so when I washed my face and brushed my teeth every morning and evening, I was reminded that I needed to make my daily confession.

People in church were not only attacking my family from the outside; the church, in my mind, was also destroying our internal infrastructure. My parents fought with each other constantly, real fights, knock down, bullets flying fights. My mother would wear dark sunglasses to church on Sunday's to shield the view of the black eyes and bruising from their altercations.

After the situation with the Baptist church, my father formed his own congregation in the Baptist denomination. He heard the message on tongues and other Word of Faith teachings and made changes. I was ten years old, the fall of 1984. He had a conversation with my sister and I, he acknowledged that the way that he treated my mother was not appropriate. He promised that there would be no more arguing and fighting between he and my mother. My father committed to change and he did. There was no more physical abuse, he and my mother rekindled their marriage.

Next, my father declared to the congregation that we were no longer Baptist. The church would drop Missionary Baptist Church from its title and reemerge the following Sunday as a Word of Faith church. Ninety-two percent of the membership left. The church membership decreased from the low hundreds to less than twenty-five. My father was not deterred, he knew that he had heard from God. He was determined to follow Him.

My father's determination paid off. He was a disciplined student of Biblical principles and theology. He studied long hours, he was always prepared when he stood before the congregation to minister. The church began to grow. People enjoyed his teachings, he was easy to understand. He was approachable. He genuinely cared. As children, we were taught to care. It was our kingdom assignment to be a blessing to others.

Whenever a member faced difficulty in life, my parents opened our home to them with complete and total access. If a member was in need they knew that immediate help would come if they called on Pastor. There was a member who fell behind on his rent and was evicted, my parents allowed him to move into our home. He lived with us for at least six months. Another member and her husband were having marital problems, my parents allowed her to move into our home, this time, I had to give up my bedroom. The member was so grateful that my parents had extended our home to her that she made my younger sister and I a crocheted skirt and matching vest set. The skirt and vest set was yellow, orange, green and blue. My mother made us wear the outfit to school so that we would not hurt the members' feelings. When I appealed to my mother's sensibility and said, "I can't wear that, I have a reputation, people will laugh at me." My mother said, "Persecution is a part of being in the first family, you only have to wear it once."

In the late 80's my father relocated the church from its location to a building on the other side of town. Unlike the last big announcement, this time the majority of the membership followed him. In the new location, the church continued to grow and it grew quickly.

My father was a pastor for the people. He was authentic and his message was fresh. He cared about every member of his church. He made certain that he always made himself available to every member. Before each church service, he would walk down the hall as people stood in line to get into the sanctuary and greet everyone. As the church membership increased, the line to talk to Pastor after service grew longer. He made an adjustment, he got a chair so he did not have to stand for so long.

He was a visionary. He was smart. He was a planner. He wrote his vision down and made it plain for members to understand. Whenever an announcement or change of any kind was forthcoming, my father would prepare the membership for the declaration by preaching Biblical principles regarding the announcement in the weeks leading up to the revealing moment.

My father's teaching were so dynamic and his delivery so charismatic, that the church attracted people from all socioeconomic backgrounds. I invited my boyfriend to church one Sunday and was surprised when he and all three of his homeboys walked up to the front when my father extended the invitation to rededicate your life to Christ. They continued to attend Sunday service and would even arrive earlier than me. In all honesty, my father's message had that affect on people. There was light in the way that he delivered the gospel, he made it simple; God made it life changing.

The church was a place where people were free to worship; it was a place for the family, it was a place for blessing. My father had successfully reestablished himself. He had built a church that no one could put him out of.

Credit

I was thirteen years old when I learned that I had major credit cards. By fifteen, I was a gold card member. At seventeen, I was certified platinum. My mother set up my credit profile. I had department store credit cards and major credit cards. My new credit file was the vehicle that my parents would use to rebuild their old damaged credit files. My credit gave them a "fresh start."

The growth of the church allowed my parents to regain their financial footing. Money was flowing in weekly and the consistent cash flow created financial stability. My father preached about his journey of faith and prosperity. He joked that at one time he and my mother were so broke that they "could not buy bubble gum on credit." They may not have been able to buy bubble gum, but I could. My mother applied for credit cards using my name and my social security number. Then, she would add herself and my father as additional cardholders. By making timely payments for charges on my credit cards, my parents increased their credit rating as additional cardholders. Of course this was back in the day before the new millennium when credit scoring rules changed.

It would take time to build my credit file but by age 17, my credit worthiness was equivalent to any responsible adults. I had corporate credit cards and personal credit cards. I was aware that I had credit cards in my name because like any other child, I was always looking for mail to come in my name. I would check the mail, rip open the envelopes addressed to me, only to be disappointed when I saw new credit cards and pre-approved credit card offers.

I had some cards with credit limits and others without credit limits. Some credit cards imprinted with my name personally and some imprinted with various business names that my parents had DBA's for, including the church.

A pre approved business credit offer was delivered to the church in an envelope addressed to me. It was an account that as the primary cardholder, I could carry an unlimited number of additional cardholders. This was not just a small business corporate credit card offer, this was a credit card offer generated from my parents spending habits on my other accounts with the credit card issuer. There were open credit accounts with the card issuer in other business names that my mother had acquired when I was younger however, the terms of those cards were different from this new offer. This particular credit card would have no credit limit and would allow my parents to add critical staff members as additional cardholders. My mother completed the credit offer using my data and I signed the completed application. Within days, new corporate credit cards started arriving for accounting, management and pastoral staff members.

The benefits of the new business credit card account included lessening the strain on cash; purchases could be made and payment would not be due for at least 30 days. In the long term, the credit card would aid in establishing business credit. The credit card would also allow for better control of spending. The reports and analytics available from the credit card issuer on spending patterns would be a valuable tool for the church.

Credit was the crux of the ministry. When offerings were down or in the summer months when giving was slow, credit allowed the church to stay on track with paying expenses. Cash was used for items that could not be paid by credit card. Things like car payments, mortgages and installment loan payments. My parents taught me how to use credit to balance inconsistent revenue.

My parents guarded their credit, they made their credit a priority. Since some of their credit was attached to my credit, my credit was a priority as well. Secretaries had been reassigned and even lost their jobs for failing to mail off credit card payments on time. Before websites and the internet made it possible for people to monitor their credit files, my mother would write every 90 days for a copy of her credit report. Credit was critical to our lives. A good credit score validated my father's message on his personal integrity, it also increased the strength of my father's signature. Credit opened doors and expanded opportunities.

When I was around 22, I received a phone call from my mother, she and one of the staff members credit cards had been declined when attempting to charge a purchase. My mother called the credit card company acting as if she were me and was advised that the card had been restricted because the payment on a personal credit card that my husband and I had through the credit card issuer was late. Since I was the primary cardholder on the church's credit card and one of my accounts was late, all charges on the other cards would be declined until payment was received. My mother was not happy that she had been "financially embarrassed." She said it was critical that I pay my bills timely since nonpayment would affect the church's ability to use the credit cards. Since I was being negligent with the payment on that card, I needed to bring the bills to her. My mother never asked if financial difficulties were preventing me from making timely payments. She wanted my bills that affected her credit privileges paid on time. It seemed like access to my credit was more important than I was.

My First Job

I graduated from high school when I was 17 years old. I spent the summer following graduation contemplating my college options and eventually settled on a university in the city. The church was steadily growing and my parents were financially well off enough to pay my college tuition without loans or grants.

My mother decided that I was not going to work. I needed to focus on my education but at the same time I needed to establish my independence. She advised me that she would provide me with a weekly allowance. I would need to use that money to pay for my clothes, gas, entertainment. She would continue to pay for my food, shelter and hair appointments. In return for the allowance I needed to make sure that my baby sister was dropped off and picked up from school everyday.

The deal was agreeable to me, the dollar amount was small, but still a lot of money in 1991 for a teenager with a brand new car and no responsibilities. One morning, before leaving for school, I walked into my parents bedroom and asked my mother for my weekly check. She gave me the check and I left.

Later that day, my mother advised me that my father was not in agreement with her giving me a weekly allowance so she would not be giving me an allowance any more, but she needed me to still drop off and pick up my baby sister from school. Also, I needed to figure out how I was going to take care of myself.

At first it did not even matter, I had a little money saved. I called my husband, who was my boyfriend at the time. I was playing around with him and I said, "I need you to give me an allowance every week." Of course he laughed and then asked me "Why?" I explained to him that my mother was cutting off my allowance and I needed money.

My boyfriend's response was "Tell them to give you your check from your *(real)* daddy." I said, "I don't get a check from my daddy, now are you going to give me the money or not?" He laughed again and said "No I am not but you get a check every month. If your daddy died and he was in the military, you get a social security payment every month." I was clueless as to what he was talking about. I had never heard of a social security payment for me or anyone else. My boyfriend said, "Go downstairs and tell them that if they aren't going to give you any money, then they need to give you your check. You are only 17 so you have at least 12 more months of checks coming."

I still had no clue what a social security check was but I had just enough information to be dangerous. My father was the only parent at home so I went to go talk to him. I explained to him that since I had to take care of myself and I did not have a job, I needed my social security check. From the look on his face, I knew I had just said the wrong thing. My father said that I needed to speak with my mother.

My mother was home within fifteen minutes, she immediately tore into me. You would swear that I had denounced Jesus. My mother went on and on about how ungrateful I was, how dare I ask my father for a check when he had taken care of me all of my life. I let her rant, I still wasn't sure if I received a social security check and I wanted to know the truth. After I was sure that my mother was finished with her tirade, I calmly asked "So do I get a social security check or not?" Since I had not ever been one to challenge my parents, my mother was visibly shocked. She paused, she confirmed that I did receive a monthly check, then she added "It ain't nothing but some change, if you want it that bad, you can have it."

I did not want the check, I just wanted my mother to tell the truth. I told her that I did not want it and walked away. I was not trying to upset either of my parents. My mother was right and I felt guilty for charging my father up over the check after all that he had given me.

The next day, my mother informed me that she would give me a reduced allowance every week. I would get a little less money than I previously received and if I wanted more than that I could come work at the church. I was still feeling like I should not have demanded to get my social security check. I did not want to continue to go through the check war with my parents. Receiving a check from my parents every week was not truly establishing my independence. I elected to work at the church.

My first position at the church was a data entry specialist. I made a little more than minimum wage and I worked part-time hours so that I could continue my college education. Promotions came rather quickly. I learned the business at a rapid pace. My father would spend countless hours with me; pouring into me his wisdom, knowledge and experience. In retrospect, I realize that he was putting me through his own mentorship program. He was molding me into the employee that he needed me to be. My father taught me to leverage the preparation and planning skills that he introduced to me as a child into my work. I was indoctrinated into my father's way of thinking. It was a painful process. I worked hard at pushing myself to be an irreplaceable help to my father. I wanted so badly to make him proud.

There were times in the beginning, when I thought that I would fail. I made up in my mind that if I did not succeed in meeting his expectations, I would fail trying. He pushed me to see how much I could take. I had various assignments, including writing outbound correspondence from my father. I read old letters that he had written just so I could adapt my writing style to his. When I presented the first draft of letters and memos that he asked me to write, he would say, "Is this your best work?" I would respond with, "I think so." He would say, "Go work on it again and come back when you are sure." He marked my drafts up with changes in a red, felt tip pen. I hated that pen. It was like being graded, but I was determined to give my father a document that he could not find an error with. Eventually, my writing met my father's approval and he would look at my work and say, "Run with it."

After a year and a few months of working at the church and going to school full-time, I decided to drop out of college. I was barely 18 years old, but my parents allowed me to come and work full time in the family business [the church]. They should have made me stay in college. I was smart and I learned new things quickly. Having a college degree would have enhanced the skill set that I had to offer our growing family business. There was no push for me to stay in college, there was no lengthy discussion. I said I did not want to go back, my parents agreed.

A few months later, my boyfriend and I were engaged. In the beginning, my parents were not overly ecstatic about the news. My father tried his best to convince me to wait 3 more years. I compromised at 18 months. When my mother learned of my engagement, she turned and walked away. They would eventually come around and see things my way. They recognized that I was not going to be disuaded.

A year and a half later I was married. I would have been happy with a simple, elegant wedding. My mother made sure that I had the wedding of her dreams. It was over the top in so many ways. Four months after we were married, my husband joined the staff of the church working in the family business.

The Business of Church

There is a sociological theory that people have a need to belong; an innate desire to form and maintain interpersonal relationships. People generally fill that need in three distinct areas of their life. The first area is through family relationships. The second is through their careers and/or jobs. The third is generally through some type of group setting. My father understood that theory and the business of the church was to ensure that our church filled the void in the third area.

There was always some sort of activity going on at the church; Conferences, Noon Bible Study, Weekday Service, Weeknight Service and Saturday Morning Service. The numerous services allowed multiple opportunities for visitors to come and experience the church. People joined the church in massive numbers. The church was the "it" place to be. It was where recent and old members gathered with their new "circle of friends."

As the church grew so did my father's ego. There was a paradigm shift in his behavior and his response to others. A new layer of my father's personality was exposed as the church, its presence, its bank accounts and staff grew.

By the time I was 19, I was promoted to Executive Administrative Assistant, I was also a newlywed. The job title suggests that I was my father's secretary, I was not. I did not schedule appointments or keep up with his calendar. My position was more of an oversight role, I was the eyes and ears for my parents while they were away from the office. I handled the personal information that my parents did not want others to see like church bank accounts that were restricted for their use, payroll and their personal bills. I took care of things for my parents. No matter how big or small.

At 21, my position had evolved to complete oversight of the day to day activities of the ministry. My position was a dual role that included Director of Human Resources and Executive Administrative Assistant. I held a seat on the church's Corporate Board of Directors, I was the Corporate Secretary. My father and my mother were the other two Board Members. My mother and I shared equal minority voting power, my father was the majority with 51% of the power.

My father would parade a group of "leaders" in front of the church and say, "This is my Advisory Board, this is the core group of people that I go to for counsel on decisions regarding the ministry." From that statement the average person concludes that the people who sat on the Advisory Board had some sort of voting power regarding church affairs. Further, that the Advisory Board was the equivalent to a corporation's Board of Directors. That was the perception. The reality was that the Advisory Board had no voting power, in fact, they had no power at all. They were a group of people that my father shared his upcoming plans with after he had already made his decision. They were his "sounding board." The truth was that there was one Corporate Board of Directors for the church. The Board of Directors consisted of three people, my father, my mother and I. The three person Board of Directors was listed in the Articles of Incorporation as the only people with any type of voting or decision making power.

As the church membership grew, so did the number of people coming to church wanting to sit under my father's wisdom before branching out to their own fellowship. From the beginning, he was always so disapproving. If ministers in the church said they were called to be Pastors and spoke to my father about him blessing them to leave the church, he rarely complied. He was extremely territorial and viewed anyone who was not willing to stay in his church and serve under him as a potential threat to split the church and take members with them. Almost with certainty that was never the person's intention. However, he was unwilling to accept the possibility that others were called.

There was a time when one of the young ministers in the church decided that he was going to start his own ministry. My father gave him a list of rules:

- His church could not be within a certain radius of any of the church facilities
- He could not discuss with others in the church that he was starting his own ministry
- His family should not be encouraged to leave my father's church to join his

When the young minister was unwillingly to comply, my father met with his mother and father and advised them that they should not have a relationship with their son because he was toxic.

"Toxic" is one of my father's buzzwords. The word carries a negative connotation without a need for further explanation. When a person uses the word toxic, I always think of those green circular stickers that I used to get in elementary school when the fire department came to visit and teach about staying away from dangerous chemicals. It is the word that my father would use whenever he felt that someone needed to be discredited and he had no other visible means of discrediting them. The word toxic immediately conjures up negative thoughts of warning, danger, poison, death. My father knew that and the word "toxic" alone served his intentions. To guard his own reputation, my father would poke holes in other people's reputation, in spite of the contributions that they made to the church ministry. He would then step aside and allow public opinion and rumors spread in an attempt to destroy the person.

The scenario with minister's in the church wanting to create their own church group would play out in the same manner over and over again. My father would map out his strategic stipulations, the minister's would disagree. The campaign from the pulpit to discredit the minister was immediate; it was an attempt to keep the membership from flocking to the new church body.

When the ministry outgrew its new location and began to expand and build new worship facilities, my father created a construction company that would act as the general contractor for all construction. I was the owner of the construction company. When the church received funding from banks for building projects, I would sign the loan documents as the Secretary of the church corporation as well as the Owner of the construction company completing the work. I was the owner in name only and for documentation purposes only, I received no compensation as the owner.

The continued growth made it necessary for my father to add staff ministers, he sought out ministers that would add to his ministry gift and bless others. He was a visionary and it was critical that everyone around him was an extension of and fully supportive of the vision that God had given him.

My father would not be upstaged, if it appeared that members in the church were increasingly engaged by the ministry of a staff minister, he would make an adjustment to move the minister to a less visible role.

When one of the Assistant Pastors preached a sermon during a weekly Bible Study that sold more tapes than my father had ever sold, instead of being happy that the minister had brought forth a message that blessed the church body. My father was visibly upset and anytime anyone in the family mentioned the sales, he would attempt to downplay the achievement.

In 1998, my job title changed to Executive Administrator, I was officially third in command of the church operations and church staff. I was 24. Even though, I held the highest ranking position underneath my father and my mother, I was never the highest paid person on staff. There were at a minimum, six staff people whose salary packages and benefits were more lucrative than mine. When I questioned, my father about my salary, he would say, "Every team needs a good coach. You are the coach, you orchestrate the activities of the team. Just like any team, there are going to players who make more money than the coach." Even though there were many perks that I received as a result of my relationship and my role, I worked hard to prove to my father that I was just as worthy of the salary that he approved for others.

Proving myself was not easy. There was always some sort of struggle for power with adults who were older than me and did not consider my decisions to be final. If situations were escalated to my father, I had a 50:50 chance of him backing up my decision. Among other things, he was a puppet-master, my father would pull the strings to play me against other staff people. He was always in control, he indirectly controlled the outcome of all situations. In the end, he would appear blameless, I would appear unreasonable.

I was assigned the task of refurnishing all the corporate offices. I had a budget, but my father gave me free reign to make decisions on the decor. I chose the furnishings for all offices, making sure that all managers had the same office furniture, so as not to create any unintentional contention. I reviewed the furnishings with my father and he approved. There was one particular staff person who did not like the furniture that I chose, she wanted something different for her office. I could have given her a budget and let her choose whatever she wanted as long as it was in budget. I did not want to do that. I advised my father of her contesting my furniture choice, he said it did not matter and advised that I should move forward with my choice. His backing was all I needed, I could assert my authority and tell her, "No." The staff member decided that she would go to my father and ask him directly to allow her to select the furniture of her choice. She was not even in his office for ten minutes before she came to me and said, "Pastor said that I can have the furniture that I selected."

    I could not believe it, my father had turned on me. He pushed me to push back on her about her choice repeatedly, even saying, that the decision was mine alone. Then he changes to her side in less than ten minutes. The result, I just looked like I was being mean and unwilling to compromise, which was definitely not the case. I cared less what furniture was selected, my goal was to stay in budget and not have any one employee feeling slighted over the furniture choices that others were allowed to make.

    The furniture issue was just one of many times where I was faced with a conflicting message from my father. It would happen time and time again. It was frustrating, but he was the boss, I had to adjust to his method, even if the method was manipulative madness.

Cars, Planes and Helicopters

By 1994, the church was expanding and growing in ways that my parents could never have imagined. There were two locations in the same city. It became necessary for my father to seek out people and things to help him manage the four Sunday morning worship services between the two locations. He added additional pastoral staff and the ministry obtained a helicopter to transport my father and my mother between the two locations.

My father's "circle of influence" increased. He booked numerous speaking engagements at churches all over the country. When the travel restraints of commercial airlines became too much of a hassle, the ministry bought a private jet and hired two full-time airline pilots.

My parents net worth was increasing dramatically. They owned several rental properties, two of which my older sister and I lived in, but not for free, our parents were also our landlords, we paid rent. They were blessed and they shared their blessings with others. They would buy cars for family members and staff and allow the person to repay the car loan through payroll deductions. They leased their rental properties to employees and family members.

As a family we dined in the finest restaurants, we wore designer clothes, we travelled in style. My mother would always remind us often that we all had to look prosperous. "Lifestyles of the Rich and Famous" meet "Lifestyles of the Rich and Religious." There was a new emergence of wealthy people in this nation, it was the megachurch Pastor. The church was making my parents wealthy, my sisters and I were "baby ballers." My father made sure we all knew, he was rich, we were just along for the ride.

My mother was a "fashionista" long before the term became popular. In 1999, when my parents moved into their newly constructed home, my mother's closet was positioned where the original blueprints were designed for a six car garage. Her closet was better than the girl in the blockbuster movie, her closet was huge and arranged by color. She had her own personal salesperson in each of the finest department stores in the city. My mother would call us if she thought we were near or in a mall, she always needed someone to pick up her clothes from the mall, thousands of dollars worth of clothes. "How are we supposed to pay for this?" My mother would reply, "You have a credit card, don't you?"

My parents drove fine cars. They had Mercedes', a Rolls Royce, SUV's, several ATV's, boats and a lake house to dock the boats. As a family we vacationed once a year in exotic places with the very best accommodations. We sailed the high seas. My parents always had to have the very best there was to offer, no matter the cost, no matter where we were. As their children, my sisters and I had access to all of that.

The accumulation of wealth opened doors of opportunity, new business ventures. My father tried venture capitalism, he would invest in other people's businesses. He tried the stock market, it would expand his financial portfolio.

My parents vacationed at least once per quarter. We would travel together as a family at least once annually. Even on vacations, I worked. I was the unofficial family travel coordinator. Most of our vacations began on a Monday and ended on Saturday so that the entire family would not have to miss Sunday service. There were times when my sisters, our spouses and children would leave the city ahead of my parents so that I could get everything settled before their arrival.

My father used the time alone with us on family vacation to map out the plan for the church the next year. After the kids were asleep, the adults would meet to discuss strategy for achieving the vision and goals for the church. Working on church business while on vacation equals deductible business expense.

The week before we were scheduled to leave for summer vacation one year, my parents decided that they wanted to alter their travel date and travel the same day as the rest of the family. They would leave after church on Sunday instead of waiting until Monday. I called the travel agent, I needed to update their reservation to arrive a day earlier. The hotel where we were staying was completely booked. The only option that the travel agent had was to book my parents in a comparable, neighboring hotel for one night and then they could move to the hotel with the rest of the family the following day, which was the arrival date of their original reservation. I needed two rooms, my younger sister would be delaying her travel until after service on Sunday and would arrive on the island with my parents.

My older sister and her family, my husband and our children and my baby sister all travelled to the island on Saturday on a commercial flight, we filled every seat in the first class cabin. As usual, I got everyone checked into the hotel and settled in. Around 11:30 p.m. I received a call from my mother,

"Kermeshea, we are here, I cannot stay in this hotel, did the travel agent tell you that it didn't have air conditioning in the rooms, the rooms all have open windows."

"No she did not tell me that, she said it was a comparable hotel."

"You have to do something, we cannot stay here, can you call the hotel you are in and see if they have any available rooms?"

"Okay, I will call you right back"

I called the hotel reservation line, it was a weekend and after hours, I knew the travel agency was not open. The hotel was booked and there were no available rooms.

I called my mother back, she had already checked everyone out of the hotel she was in, she was not staying there. I explained to her that there were no rooms available. The hotel was booked. My father got on the phone, "Poom, why didn't you check this hotel out before we got here, I can't stay here, I would rather sleep on my jet." "Daddy, the travel agent said the hotel was fine, I don't understand why you are having issues."

My husband overheard the conversation and said call our credit card company. He was absolutely right, I don't know why I had not thought of it. Since I had been a cardholder for one particular credit card company since I was a teenager, our joint credit card had a 24 hour Travel Line that cardholders could call if they were stranded anywhere in the world. You know the saying, "Membership Has Its Privileges." I told my father to give me five minutes and I would call him back, I was sure I could work something out and he would not have to spend the night on his jet.

I called the credit card company, I had to act as if I was stranded. I explained to the representative that my hotel accommodations had not panned out, I needed two rooms in the hotel where we would all be staying for the week. I was placed on a brief hold and the representative returned to the line advising that my reservation was confirmed. The Front Desk Manager would have keys waiting for me when I arrived, I just needed to show the Front Desk Manager my credit card.

I called my father back and advised him that I had secured two rooms and I would meet them in the lobby of the hotel.

When my parents arrived my father was in a mood, my mother was just glad she would not have to sleep in the heat. My father said, "Now how is it that one minute the hotel does not have any available rooms and the next minute you have not one, but two suites booked?" I explained to my father that it was the type of credit card that we had, we were valued cardholders and one of the benefits was emergency travel services. Hotels hold rooms vacant for situations like this and the credit card company had the relationship connection with the hotel that I did not, so they were able to secure the rooms. My father wanted to know how he could get his own credit card with similar privileges. I explained to them that my credit card had to be used to pay for the room and would remain on the room for any incidental charges. My mother wanted to know why, I said, "I don't know that was their rules, does it matter? It all gets paid the same way." My mother agreed. We all said good night, finally after a day full of travel I could go to sleep.

A New Arrival

"Your sister is pregnant"
"Okay she is married, what is wrong with you?"
"No, not that sister, your younger sister"
"Oh! Wow"

I had just walked into my parents home. I was greeted by mother. Obviously, agitated, no it was greater than agitated, she was mad.

In three days, my parents were leaving for a 14 day trip to the Holy Land. The call came that morning from someone who did not leave a name. The caller said. "Your daughter is pregnant and she is afraid to tell you," before disconnecting the call. My younger sister was away at college. My mother called her and she confirmed that she was indeed pregnant.

My younger sister arrived home the next day, that night we had a family meeting. My father began the meeting explaining that my younger sister could not be an unwed mother and live in his house. Which one of us, my older sister or me, was going to take care of the baby? My older sister already had two children so she wasn't jumping at the opportunity to add one more. After a lengthy discussion, I said, "Why can't she take care of her own baby?" My father explained that the situation was not good from an appearance perspective.

I turned to my younger sister, I realized that everyone was talking around her like she was not in the room. I said, "What do you want to do?" She didn't know, she was young and confused. My father would go on to say that she made a terrible choice, even after he had warned her not to. She could not live with him, she needed to get out.

❖

I looked at my mother, knowing that she knew all too well the loneliness and failure that my younger sister had to have been feeling at that point. My mother had walked in her shoes, her parents did not put her out. She said nothing, she was more concerned about how the teenage pregnancy would affect her image than she was about caring for her own daughter.

I said to my sister, "I haven't talked to *my husband* but I am sure that you can stay with me. You can stay as long as you need to." I turned to my parents and let them know how wrong they were, how disappointed I was in their response. Neither of them were moved.

My parents left for their trip to Jerusalem. They called during the trip to check on the affairs of the church, they never asked about the welfare of my younger sister, so I would just tell them. As long as I had their ear, they were not going to ignore her for nine months.

When they returned from their trip, my father had apparently experienced some type of epiphany in the Holy Land. He returned with a message on choices. He taught about choices that children make and the parental responsibility. The message on choices encompassed teaching on teenagers making the choice to live a life holy before God. He encouraged parents to bring their teens to church to hear the message. My younger sister was not visibly pregnant but my father was preparing the membership for the news of her pregnancy.

The series on choices ended with a commitment ceremony where parents and their teenagers exchanged rings and the teens made a vow to live holy. It was touching.

My mother continued to struggle with how people would perceive her because of my sister's pregnancy. When it was time to plan a baby shower, my mother said that I should host the shower. There were rules of course, she would attend but do not include her name on the invitations as a host. She did not want it to appear that she was endorsing my younger sister's choices.

When my younger sister gave birth, my mother was there. I was just happy to see that both she and my father had accepted that the baby was coming, whether they liked it or not.

Ministry

As a child, I saw church as a place that I spent most of my time. God was my parents deal and I would find Him when the time was right. That's not to say that I was not saved. I was, I accepted Jesus Christ as my Lord and Saviour and was baptized at an early age. I just was not one of those radical, sold out for Jesus teenagers. I knew right from wrong and never really strayed away from the right thing to do.

When I initially started to work for the church, instead of just being church; church would become church and my job. In my early twenties, I started to see the difference in church and ministry. Church was the building, ministry was the impact that the services in the building had on others. My father and I did not always see eye-to-eye on ministry. As I matured, the blending of business, church and ministry in my mind would become a conflict to the separation of three in my father's mind.

I thought of ministry as my purpose. All the years of my father's teachings on walking into your purpose, the lessons from my childhood, the instructions from my youth came together in my mind and my view of church would change from church being a building to church being an outreach for blessing people's lives. My father was blessed with a successful church. I felt that the ministry was the avenue by which our family would bless others.

My husband was significant in opening my eyes to ministry. When my father would ask me to carry out tasks that I did not agree with, my position was that it was my job, he is my boss; while I am at work, I am here to do whatever he asks me to do. My husband's thought process was significantly different. He would say, "Kermeshea at some point you have to have a conscious." He would go on to say, "You cannot treat people any kind of way just because your daddy says to."

  He was right, at times, I was cold when I should have been compassionate. I had a quick temper, I went from zero to sixty, without warning, full throttle ahead. I did not like to be challenged. I was unapproachable and guarded. I was "hot" and "cold" my attitude adjusted based on the events that transpired during the day. I have a natural look in my face that at times is intimidating; I knew it and I used "the look" to show my displeasure. There were some people that I just did not like, and I had no issues with letting them know that. Instead of me accepting people as they were, they had to prove to me that they were worthy. A large part of my personality was who I was raised to be. But, I was an adult, I should not have needed my husband to remind me that I was not treating people appropriately. I had little regard for the lesson that we all learn in Kindergarten, "Do unto others as you would have them do unto you."

  My husband was raised in the Methodist church. He joined my family's church not long after we began dating. Often times, my husband would sit in silent disagreement with decisions that were made. He felt it was not his place to challenge the issue. But, he had no reservations about challenging me.

  Around 4:30 a.m. one morning, my home phone rang. It was my husband, he had been at the church working all night preparing for an upcoming conference. He did not normally call home while working late nights because he knew that the kids were sleeping and the phone would wake them up. When I heard his voice, I knew something was wrong.

  My husband had just received a call from one of his staff members. This particular person had been a member of the church for a while. The staff member called my husband to let him know that he would not be able to report to work for the conference. He had been smoking crack, his wife wanted him to check into a rehabilitation facility. After encouraging the employee to stay focused on his recovery, my husband called me.

I listened. I could hear the disappointment in my husband's voice. The more details my husband provided, the sadder I felt. I was sad for the employee, his wife, his kids. Since the ministry had a drug rehabilitation center, my husband asked me to do him a favor and make room for this employee. Most likely all the beds that we had in the rehab center were full, I would have to make special accommodations. I knew it was the right thing to do. I agreed that I would contact the manager of the center once I thought he was awake. I gave my husband a list of the items that I could remember that the employee would need to bring with him at check-in.

My husband had one additional request, he wanted me to allow him to hold the employee's position until he completed the rehabilitation program. I agreed to hold the job.

Later that morning, I had a conversation with my father to bring him current regarding the events surrounding the employee. Needless to say, my father was livid that I had agreed to allow the employee into the rehabilitation center and to hold his job. My opinion was that we were a church, positioned to be a blessing to the Body of Christ. Seemingly, my father had another opinion.

My husband and I would both have to stand together to convince my father that the church's drug rehabilitation center was the right place for the employee to go. My father wanted the employee to go to a facility in another city. My husband reminded him that the program at the church was faith based, it was free, it was proven. The program would afford the employee the opportunity to be near his children. The employee would be able to get the help that he needed right here in our city.

Next, we discussed holding the employee's job. I had never held a job at any other company, but I knew from HR magazines that companies had employee assistance programs that allowed their employees to seek rehabilitative and mental health service in time of need while providing anonymity as well as job security. I explained to my father that as a church ministry, we should be better than the world. We have the resources available to us to positively affect the employee's recovery. We would be remiss in our responsibility if we were to dismiss him and not keep his job open.

Reluctantly my father agreed and the employee was allowed to return to his job after completing the 90-day program.

To me this situation was just one segment of ministry, being there for the people who needed you at their time of need. My father would recognize my passion for the church, and my compassion for others. Though he and I did not always agree, for a time, my father did allow me the freedom to increase the ministry's outreach programs as I saw fit. Most people never knew that I was behind the scenes pushing for certain things. My exterior was all about business but my heart was for affecting change in people's lives.

I worked diligently to revamp the areas that affected the next generation. I remembered the church activities that excited me as a child and I was committed to bringing those type of activities back to the church. I concentrated my efforts and focus into Children's Ministry, Youth Ministry and to establishing programs within the church that ministered to the needs of the entire congregation. I didn't need to be out front to let everyone know that I was in charge. I was content to see my work and creativity come to fruition and know that there was a positive affect on other lives.

    The ministry itself was blossoming. There was barely enough room to accommodate all the people in the worship services. The church staff worked hard to make it happen. The hours were long, more than fourteen most days. The lines between church the job and church the ministry started to blur. The staff worked seven day weeks. Everyone was committed to the church and their jobs. It was our purpose, it was what God had called us to do. This was ministry.

Church Gossip

There is this unspoken, unseen pressure associated with being in the First Family. Everything that is said, everything that you do, how you wear your hair, the clothes you wear; the simplest things are all subject to intense scrutiny. Next to beauty and barber shop gossip, church gossip is the worse. Church gossip for the Pastor's family is almost like a cancer.

The First Family in a church is often the subject of church gossip. Everyone has an opinion about how the children should be raised, what the children are doing, where the children are going. The pastor and his family have the unsolicited honor of hearing church gossip and the task of discrediting church gossip.

People in the church will masquerade gossip as concern. You know how it goes, "I am concerned about Sis. Whatever, I think her and her husband are having problems." Why do you think that? "Oh I don't want to say, I just heard some things from Bro. Whoever, Girl we just need to pray."

Growing up my father would always tell my sisters and I, don't listen to everything that everyone in the church tells you. People want to take your place so they will lie to you to make you doubt the things that I say to you.

As a child, church gossip made me very distrusting of people. At a very young age, church gossip betrayed my confidence in others to do the right thing. But it also made me overprotective of my family. My mother would often refer to me as "the glue." People knew I would not tolerate you talking about my family. I didn't let my family talk about each other. I was determined to hold us together and not let words tear us apart.

To me, family protected one another. To my father, family had become a built in workforce to expand his dream. My father did not always heed the words of advice that he would so often give to my sisters and I. He listened to church gossip, he believed church gossip.

As a teenager, I would go to church on Sunday's with the expectation that I would have to defend myself against some unfounded accusation when I got home. Kermeshea said this, Kermeshea did that. I saw the impact of church gossip first hand and the results were never good for anyone involved. I saw families destroyed, people rejected, friendships betrayed; all because of church gossip.

My father's belief of church gossip became the loose thread in the fabric of my trust in him. It started to unravel my comfort in his ability to handle things fairly. A little while after my fifth wedding anniversary, a member of the church made a "concerned" call to my father one night to advise him that my husband was having an affair with one of his female coworkers. Without research or inquiry, he believed the member's accusations. That evening, my father contacted one of the manager's at the church and advised her that he would be firing my husband the following day and she needed to take over his responsibilities. He arrived in the office the next morning and called my husband over for a meeting. He began the meeting advising my husband that, "he knew" and "his secret was exposed." The conversation continued and my father advised my husband of the details of the member's phone call. When my husband denied the accusations, my father explained that the member provided the name of the female coworker and stated that he saw a truck like my husband's pick the female up from work the prior week to take her to lunch. My husband immediately recognized the female's name, it was his ex-girlfriend; he advised my father that he needed to bring me into the conversation. When I entered the office, my father explained the situation and asked if I knew the female. I confirmed that I did and explained to him that she was delusional among other things.

My father still was not convinced, so I advised him to bring my older sister to the conversation. My older sister was aware of many of the events that had transpired over the years with the female, that I had not shared with my parents. She confirmed the same things that both my husband and I had explained. The three of us questioned my father's judgement, how is it that he considered the members' accusations to be truth based on a truck that, "looked like" my husband's picking someone up from work? Additionally, we all worked through lunch and often had someone bring our lunch into the office. When would my husband have found time during the day to drive across town to pick someone up for lunch and not be missed? At the time, my husband drove a white SUV with factory rims and tires. Car dealerships sell white SUV's multiple times everyday of the week, his truck was not unique. I asked, "Did the member confirm that he saw the person driving the truck?" My father replied,"Well no, he just thought he recognized the truck because the female had pictures of herself and [*my husband*] in high school in a photo album that she brought to work." Photos from high school. Really?

Once my father was convinced that the member's "concern" was not valid, he said to my husband, "Okay, you can go back to work." My husband and I both inquired whether he was going to call the member and advise that the information that he provided was not truth, my father replied, "Ya'll can call him, it's just mess, I don't want to be involved." I explained to my father that the member called him and based on the actions that he had taken last night and that morning towards belief that my husband was guilty, I thought that he should make the call to clear things up. My father disagreed and said that I could look up the member's phone number in the membership files if I wanted to speak to him.

At a minimum, my father's haste to believe my husband's guilt was disturbing to me. When the gossip was disproved, all of a sudden it was mess, but less than 24 hours before it was valid enough to warrant initiating staffing adjustments. I knew that my father wanted to believe the gossip. Why? The gossip presented an opportunity for him to regain control of one of his girls.

Growing up my parents always had different "preacher friends." Some would be friends for a season, some would be friends over time. One particular pastor friend and his wife were my parents friends over time. Our families spent a great deal of time together. When my father was a struggling Baptist minister we would eat and stay at their home more than once. When my father joined the Word of Faith movement and began to minister and teach on things that fell outside of the Baptist religion teaching philosophy, their relationship became strained. The pastor friend and his wife relocated to another city and lost touch for a while. Later, after I was married, my parents rebuilt their relationship with the couple. The pastor friend and his wife moved back to our city and he joined the church staff as an Assistant Pastor.

A couple from the church made an appointment to speak with my father for counseling. During the counseling session, the couple revealed to my father that they had been living in the home of the Assistant Pastor and had information to share with my father. The couple was "concerned" that the Assistant Pastor and his family did not have the First Family's interest at heart.

The couple presented my father with a typed journal they had been keeping on a daily basis while the Assistant Pastor had opened the doors of his home to them. The couple had documented all the conversations that they had heard while living in the Assistant Pastor's home.

I would have sent the couple away from me and never considered a word that they said. Who keeps a journal of other people's conversations? Furthermore, it was suspect that the couple had not included themselves and what they themselves said in the conversations.

My father was furious and sought vengeance. There was nothing in the journal that was not the truth. It just happened to be a document of truths that my father did not want to face.

My father held a meeting with the Assistant Pastor and his wife. They did not deny that any of the language was their words or thoughts. They were apologetic and recognized that they should not have allowed their thoughts to become so tainted that they would speak ill of a lifelong friend and his family. I felt their apology was sincere, my father was not convinced.

My father spent the following four days drafting a document, a Repentance and Restoration Plan for the Assistant Pastor. His Repentance and Restoration Plan's were not about rebuilding trust, they were about reminding the offender of his importance and reestablishing his power in their lives. My father would use one of his attorney's to initiate the exchange of the document. Using his attorney was a power move on his part. The document was what my father deemed necessary steps for the Assistant Pastor and his wife to convince him that they were truly apologetic and repentant and were not just saying so because they got caught. The demands in the document were mostly centered on reminding and restating for the Assistant Pastor that everything that he had was a gift from my father and my father was in absolute control. A few of the demands, the document required were:

- Giving up the home near the location where the Assistant Pastor ministered. (My father wanted to punish the Assistant Pastor. If he would continue to minister at his current assigned location, he would drive from his home 90 miles away to get there)
- The Assistant Pastor needed to give up the car that the ministry provided for his use
- The Assistant Pastor would commit to more teaching assignments at the main church location (This would require the Assistant Pastor to give up one of his scheduled off days)
- The Assistant Pastor would need to write a letter of apology (My father would later read the letter to the entire congregation at every service in every location in an attempt to discredit the Assistant Pastor)

The list went on and on, page after page. Initially, the Assistant Pastor would agree to my father's terms. The prompt agreement made my father want more, so he started to add additional terms. At which point, the Assistant Pastor walked away. My father defended his actions by saying that the relationship was toxic. When he would retell the story, he sensationalized the events to make people think the circumstances were greater than they really had been.

This was not just any staff member. This was my father's friend and they had been friend's for years, long before I was born. Instead of rising above the situation or just severing ties, my father had to prove that he was the one that God had bestowed all the blessings on. He was the one that God saw fit to entrust with this megachurch empire. He alone, could take all that he had shared with his friend away.

A few years later, another Assistant Pastor would experience a similar circumstance. A member of the church recorded conversations with him and set up an appointment with my father for him to listen to the tapes. Again, nothing that was said was untrue. He also was subjected to one of my father's Repentance and Restoration Plans.

My father did not offer Restoration Plans to all staff members, only to the ones that he felt that their absence from the ministry would cause some level of backlash. The plans were a method to silence the staff member about the situation while still making sure that they were still visible in the church. The plan gave my father an increased level of control in the person's life but also perpetuated the appearance that my father was forgiving of the situation. It was like a game of chess with people's lives. When my father felt threatened, he called a checkmate. At the end of the game, he would be the "king" left standing. It seemed to me that my father had to always prove that he was the man. He was God's chosen one. The Bible says, "Till 1 make thine enemies thy footstool" (Luke 20:43). My father was not going to wait on God, he would make his enemies crash and burn with no ember left to light. Everyone around was just enjoying the benefits of his blessings. My father was generous enough to give but he could also take away.

Holidays

Holidays were not extended family gatherings in our house growing up. It was a rare treat that I would see my extended family on Christmas or Thanksgiving. Once my parents joined the Word of Faith movement, my mother's side of the family thought my father had my mother brainwashed, "drinking the kool-aid." My father's side of the family was distant. So holidays were typically my mother, my father, my sisters and I. As adults, our spouses and children were added to the holiday table.

Spending time together as a family was enjoyable. We could spend time together and not have any major fall outs. Our family consisted of my father, my mother and my sisters; not having extended family around was not unusual. There was always this unspoken "us against the world mentality." As a child I would have loved to see my grandparents and cousins at Christmas time, but I knew better than to press the issue.

As an adult, my husband and I split Thanksgiving Day between his parents house and my parents house. Christmas morning would be spent with his relatives and Christmas Day with my family. My mother was not pleased with the Christmas plans, she preferred that we all stay the night at her house on Christmas Eve and wake up together Christmas morning. Eventually, she accepted that I would not be able to comply with her wishes.

My mother loved to give gifts, as kids our Christmas' were over the top, custom dollhouses, clothes, bikes, you name it we got it. As adults, my mother would still treat Christmas like we were still little girls. She showered our children with gifts. My mother sent my sisters and I to the toy store every year before Christmas, "buy everything that the kids want," she would say. As our children got older and understood gifts, my mother would overly indulge them with Christmas gifts. My mother believed that money was a means to show her affection.

Thanksgiving 1998, my husband and I decided that we were not going to my parents for Thanksgiving. We did not know that my older sister and her husband had made the same decision. I called on Thanksgiving Day and told my mother that we were staying home. She asked why, I blamed it on my husband, I knew she would not question that response.

The truth was my parents needed a wake up call. A conversation was not going to happen where I had their ear without me sending a strong message first. My parents need to control my life as if I were a teenager was becoming more than I could bear. I was always at the church either for work or for church service. I spent more time with my parent's during the day than I did with my husband or children. My second child was four months old and my husband's seventeen year old sister would pick both of my children up from daycare. She and my mother-in-law would feed them, bathe them, get them ready for bed and either myself or my husband would pick them up on our way home from the office. The pick up time was never earlier than 10:00 p.m.

The following Monday when we arrived at work, my father's secretary advised my older sister and our spouses that my father wanted to meet with all of us at a certain time.

The meeting began with my father saying, "Why didn't ya'll show up for Thanksgiving?' It was my first time hearing that my older sister and her husband did not go to Thanksgiving dinner. Admittedly, it was a bit amusing. Since no one answered, my younger sister decided that she would speak up. "I will tell you why no one was there. They are all tired of you trying to run their lives."

Who made her my spokesperson? She just went on and on, giving her explanation of me and my older sister's actions. When I grew tired of listening, I stopped her.

I told my parents that the reason that my husband and I did not come to Thanksgiving dinner was because we needed a break. I did not have a happy medium and I did not want the imbalance to start to taint our parent and child relationship. I was working too much. We all worked hard, I realized that, and I was not suggesting that I worked more than anyone else in the family. My work was taking over my life. My life was a repetitive cycle of church and work. Furthermore, it was becoming increasingly difficult for me to separate our relationships as parent and child and boss and employee. Their need to control was hindering my growth as an adult, as a wife and as a parent.

I went on to explain that I understood that they wanted us to have the best. However, I felt like that best was what they considered the best and not what I wanted. I was tired and I just wanted to rest and spend time with my children. There was no work/life balance. When I was at work, I was at church; when I was at church I was at work. The time just seemed to bleed together. My job was causing me to miss valuable moments raising my children. My children were growing up just like I did, with parents that they saw when they woke up in the morning, in a rush to dress them, get to work and they were sleep by the time I was able to pick them up from my mother-in-law at night.

My father gave the same explanation that he always did. My duties during church services was helps ministry and I had to learn to see my job and church as separate. That was easier said than done. I walked out of my office in one building into church in another building almost everyday of the week. Work and church was not separate to me, it was just a change of venue. He said, we needed the "Word" so we could get our hearts right. How was I supposed to make that happen? I rarely sat down for a service. My husband and I rode in separate cars to church and travelled at different intervals to the four worship services between the two worship facilities in the city.

I gave my father an example of the most recent conference. I had worked 16 to 18 hour days in the six weeks leading up to the conference. When the day of the conference finally arrived, I was already so tired from the preparation but the real work was just beginning. I told him that Thursday night of the conference when I walked into my house at 2:00 a.m. I was just so tired I was almost delirious. I said, "I was standing in the shower crying and daddy, you know I don't cry." I went on to explain that I was worn out and that tears just started to flow. My father said, "Well I don't understand that. It's just silly." He then turned to my husband and jokingly said, "What did you do to her to make her cry?"

In an attempt to help me out, my husband said, "Pastor, what I think she is trying to get you to understand is that we are all working very hard. Our staffs are drained. You take a vacation every quarter so that you can rejuvenate, we do not. We finish one big event and come back to work the next day to begin working on the next big event. We need to find a way to maintain a balance."

My father was not happy about his response. He was visibly flustered by the attack on his integrity that he perceived my husband's comments to be. Spouses were always a threat to the order and control that my father wanted for his girls. Neither mine nor my older sister's spouse grew up in the church. So neither of them viewed my father in the way that a young man who had been a part of the ministry all his life would have. He was their father-in-law first, their pastor second. Spouses were a voice of reason, a voice of logic that obstructed my father's voice.

My father explained that he was the one who had to stand before the people, he was the one that was using his faith every week to make sure we were paid. He needed a vacation to make sure that he was refreshed and ready to hear from God. We all needed to get over it.

The meeting ended with one resolution, our mother expected us to be around on holidays. My father did not want to have a conversation about that again.

Falling Apart

"Get the keys to my church from that nigga!" My father's words, from his mouth to my ears. The nigga he is referring to that would be my husband.

July 1999, by this time the church was expanding at a phenomenal rate. There were four locations in two states, two Early Childhood Development Centers, an Elementary School, a Drug Rehabilitation Center, a Bible Training Institute, all of which were my responsibility. The ministry employed more than 200 full time staff members and my husband was one of them. He was the head of the ministry's Audio and Video Departments and wholly responsible for audio and video equipment set up as well as production of the ministry's television program.

My husband and I had just walked into the house from a week long trip, traveling to each of the church locations when the phone rang. The trip from Texas to California, back to Texas and every church location in between was to make sure that the audio was working appropriately in all worship facilities.

The voice on the other end of the phone was my father. He wanted to speak to my husband. I could only hear my husband's half of the conversation, it was something like this.

"Hey Pastor, how are you doing?"
"Everything went well, you should not have any issues with your microphone during service"
"Yes, I told you about that when I first started the company"
"I guess you have selective amnesia?"
"Remember we had this conversation on the jet traveling to (that church) where you were ministering? I showed you the book that I was reading about the music industry"

"It's already started, it's already done"
"Well, I am not going to shut my company down"
"Okay"

My husband handed the phone back to me. "Get the keys to my church from that nigga!" Screamed so loud that I did not even need to have the phone receiver to my ear to hear what was said. I could not even think of my response before my husband says, "Tell that nigga, I ain't got no keys." My thoughts are going crazy, there is some real drama unfolding around me and I am clueless as to what is going on. I am thinking to myself how did this conversation go from "Hey, how are you?" to "nigga" in less than two minutes. I knew enough about their individual personalities and there was no such thing as "waving the white flag." No surrender from either side. I have to fix this.

I placed my ear on the receiver, mentally I am in recovery mode. I cannot choose sides in this conversation, I just need at least one of the two of them to tell me what is going on.

"Daddy, what keys? What are you talking about?"
"Get the keys to my church from that fool! I just fired him!"
"You fired him, what are you talking about?"

My husband interjects, "He did not fire me, I quit and I don't have nothing that belongs to him or that church."

The conversation was on the fast track to nowhere. I did the only thing that I knew to do. The thing that I had done every time before. I said, "Okay Daddy, I will take care of it." I let my father rant about thirty-seconds more and ended the conversation.

I placed the phone receiver on the base, turned to my husband and asked "What just happened?" My husband went on to explain to me that my father was upset that he had started a record label that would create and sell rap music and demanded that he immediately shut it down. When my husband said that he would not do that, the result was the part that I already knew.

So now what? I am not really even concerned about my husband. He would be fine and he had already moved on to the next phase of his life. I sat down on the bed and pulled out my planner. Now I have to figure out who is going to make sure that sound and video are set up for church tomorrow. One of the last things that my father said to me before hanging up was to make sure that my husband did not set foot on his church grounds. So not only have I lost the main staff person in charge but I have also lost the option of begging my husband to help me out as a volunteer. How am I going to explain this to the staff?

My husband walked back into the room, saw me scrambling and asked what he could do to help. He agreed that he would contact a few volunteers at all worship locations to make sure that audio and video were covered without advising them that he no longer worked for the church. I was relieved. Little did I know that my husband's departure from the church was the smallest tremble in the colossal earthquake that would shake up my life in the coming week.

The Monday following the issue with my husband and my father, I was sitting in my office, working to catch up from the previous week. My office was located near the main conference room. I heard the conference room door slam, followed by my older sister screaming, "You're wrong, you are not going to tell me what to do with my life." I didn't move, I didn't even stop working. Within seconds, my assistant was standing at the door of my office with a panicked look on her face wanting to make sure that things were okay with me. I was fine, so I told her not to worry. I had already decided that whatever was going on, would find its way to me on a need to know basis and I was not going to get involved until it became necessary.

Thirty minutes later, my mother shows up at my office door with a message "Your father wants to see you." The walk to my father's office was less than 25 steps but I felt like a dead man walking. I walked into my father's office, pen and planner in hand. Whatever had just happened could only mean one thing, I needed to make the wrong right. When I sat down my father said, "I just fired your sister and her husband." One would think that I would have seen that one coming, especially since the same thing just happened to my husband. My father went on to say, "I have told all of you girls, ain't none of ya'll going to make me lose what I got and your sister obviously doesn't understand that."

At this point, I am still trying to wrap my mind around the "I just fired" part, I was just not able to fully comprehend the word's coming out of his mouth. He went on to explain the why, apparently my older sister and her husband were living apart and chose not to tell my father. Their decision to not be completely forthcoming with him made my father angry so he fired them both.

I received my instructions, turn off their cell phones, call a locksmith to get the locks changed, collect keys, update the signature cards on the bank accounts, draft an email informing the staff. One final thing, my father informed me that he would no longer pay for my sister's two children to continue to attend the ministry's school and I needed to figure out how it would be paid. He and my mother were going to lunch and would call me later. I had no words, all I could do was move my head up and down to acknowledge that I understood his instructions.

I walked back to my office, closed and locked the door, sat down and one lonely tear made its way down my left cheek. What Now? I recognized that I had to pull myself together and keep it moving, I had business to take care of. My husband, my older sister, my brother-in-law, I love them all dearly. I depended on them daily. They were my core, the "go to" people that I trusted. There was no way for me to rationalize the events that had transpired in the last 72 hours. It was just too much for me. Clearly, my family unit was falling apart.

The next morning, my father and mother arrived at the office earlier than normal, my mother called me into her office for a family meeting. Seriously? A family meeting? Right now? In the office? At the church?

I was the last invitee to the meeting. I walked into my mother's office to find my father and younger sister waiting. The furniture had been moved around, the arrangement was not like normal. Strategically everyone else had taken their seat. My father was seated behind my mother's desk, my mother was seated to his right, my younger sister to his left. There was one chair available for me, directly in front of my father, in the middle of my mother and younger sister. I looked from person to person there was minimal eye contact, no familiar smiles. I was so unsure of the possible outcomes of the situation, all I could do was brace myself for the worse.

When I sat down, my father began to thank my younger sister for "bringing those things to his attention." He goes on to say that we need to pull together as a family and I need to make my younger sister feel comfortable as she steps up to assist me with the things that my older sister would normally do. As the conversation progresses,

I finally start to get an understanding of the initial statement of thanks to my younger sister.

Days earlier, my younger sister had gone to my father to "tell on" my husband, my older sister and my brother-in-law. My younger sister told my father that my husband was using the ministry's resources to design his business logo and that she had a "friend" who saw my brother-in-law moving furniture into an apartment.

Since my father felt like he was the last person to know, he allowed himself to believe that my husband, my brother-in-law and my older sister had intentionally conspired to deceive him. The truth was that my husband had paid one of the graphic artists who contracted work for the church to design a logo for him. My older sister and her husband had separated recently and decided not to tell either of my parents because they were trying to work things out on their own.

Instead of my father acting as parent and Pastor to my older sister and her husband and offering to counsel them through their issues, he considered them guilty of his accusations and their actions to be a deliberate attempt at deception.

I should have been shocked that the person who truly had acted deceptively was being thanked for the role she played. However, that was the backbone of our upbringing, love was gained and approval measured based on the level of information that my sisters and I were able to provide our parents on each other. The problem with this situation was we were no longer children, each of us was grown and married. Had my younger sister not considered the repercussions of her misinformation beyond the accolades that she sought in the moment that she provided the information to my father?

In my house, my husband was starting a business and we would have the income from my job. My older sister and her husband had both lost their income; as far as I knew they had no alternate plans and they had two young children to care for. I was the only person in the family meeting who was concerned about family. My father said that they should have thought about that before they "did what they did." I ended the meeting offering an update from my instructions the prior day. I would pay for my older sister's children tuition to attend the school. My father looked at my mother and informed me that my mother had convinced him that he should not stop paying his grandchildren's tuition. Was that really all the convincing that she was capable of doing?

I walked the ten steps back to my office. I sat down at my desk in the same way that I had the day before, except for this time I did not close the door. I could hear my mother, my father and my younger sister laughing and joking with one another. There I sat feeling as if I were in the belly of the beast. I felt so alone. The chatter and laughter from the office next door, became like muffled voices far away in the distance. My mind was in another place, the beat of my heart was slow and loud, my soul was sad for my older sister, my emotions were angry at my younger sister. What was I going to do? Why did God let this happen? I just sat there staring at the mesh of colors in the wallpaper on the adjacent wall.

A few minutes later, the private line in my office rang. Everyone who had access to that number was either in the office next door or not in the mood to talk. I answered the phone, thinking it was my husband. The voice on the other end was the wife of a family friend who was also a prominent Pastor in the Word of Faith movement. She said, "Hey Kermeshea, sweetheart I got an urgent message that you called crying, is everything okay?" I had not called her, I had not called anyone. So I said, "No I didn't call you." Her reply was "That is strange, maybe my secretary got the name wrong. Well, I don't want to hold you sweetheart, I love you and if you need me call me."

I hung up the phone. Now I am mad at myself. I could have gone into the details of the past week with the Pastor's wife. She would have listened, but more than that, my parent's both respected her and her husband's opinion. She could have and would have intervened. The issue that I was dealing with was family business. I had to keep it in the family. I chose to believe that the phone call was God's way of letting me know that He was there.

Later that day, while my mother was on her way home from the office, she called me. My mother wanted to thank me for never publicly humiliating her. She wanted me to know that she appreciated that I had always done exactly what my father and her asked and she appreciated that I had not grown up to be an embarrassment. What mother thanks their child for not embarrassing them? As a mother, I cannot imagine having that type of conversation with any of my children. I love them when they make me proud and would love them if they did something embarrassing. It is what mother's do, they love unconditionally. I came to realize that she needed me to know that she would not be able to overcome the embarrassment, if I did.

My father and my husband would eventually come to a place where they could be cordial with one another. In part because he needed my husband to come and fix the audio in the church again, my husband agreed to help. By that time, my husband had already decided for himself that he had no intentions of ever going back to a worship service at the church again. So he never did.

My older sister and my brother-in-law were distant from the family for months to come. They sporadically attended church, but they were attempting to rebuild their lives together.

    I would spend the next year, working at the church, partly because I felt obligated to the family business, partly because I did not know any better. Partly because I cared about the people that I worked with everyday. They had relationships with my husband, my brother-in-law and my older sister. The employees of the church were confused and hurting and I needed to be there for them.

Hopeless

In the month's that followed the family firings, I became angrier everyday. My pain had turned to being just plain pissed off. I was immature, I was a fool. In the past, I had always sided with my parents, regardless of the situation. I believed in the "us" against "them" mentality. I had become tainted, pleasing God was secondary to pleasing and protecting my parents, regardless of their actions. When my father's demands effected my "core group," I began a slow march down a "path of enlightening."

My anger would soon be replaced with hopelessness. I went to church, made sure that everything was in order while I was there, but I was not listening. I could sit through a full worship service and never hear a word that was said. I honestly, did not care. I knew how to hold it together long enough to disguise my true feelings. The only person my anger was affecting was me, I was suffering as a result of it. The people who I was angry with, had moved on.

My father, my mother, my younger sister all acted like nothing happened. It was the most dysfunctional situation that I had ever been a part of in my life. The only one of the three - my husband, my brother-in-law and my older sister - names that was ever mentioned was my husband. That was most likely because I was still around. My mother would say, "Why doesn't *(your husband)* come with you to church, you have children and you look like a single mother." I would say, "Mama, do you see this ring on my finger, no one thinks I am single, no one is even concerned about that. We have bigger concerns than the appearance of my marital status and I really don't care what people think."

My mother would plan girls day out shopping trips, Friday night family dinners and never mentioned inviting my older sister or her husband. I would decline the invitation and was shocked to see my younger sister indulged by the fact that she had alone time with my mother.

I would challenge my father, not in a disrespectful way, just more passionately than I had ever challenged him before. I was increasingly uncomfortable with the way that I was expected to treat people on his behalf. I spoke my mind and I did not hold back. My father would say, "This is my church, I am your boss, if you keep it up I am going to fire you." I think a small part of me wanted him to make good on his threat.

I tried my best to persuade my parents to let my sister come back to work. My father was not listening, he was done with my sister and wanted nothing more to do with her. When issues would come up with other staff people and my father determined that their corrective action should be less than termination, I would say, "You have to admit that the issue with (my older sister and her husband) was less egregious than this. Can they come back?" The answer remained the same, a resounding "No!"

I was planning our family vacation for the summer months. The entire family always took at least one annual vacation together. When my mother gave me the destination, I contacted the travel agent to arrange for accommodations for everyone including my older sister and her family. When I presented my father with the complete cost, he asked why my older sister was included. I responded, "Because it's a family vacation, emphasis on family." My father looked at me as if I was really trying his patience and said, "Poom, I am not paying for them to go on vacation." So I said, "Well what about the kids?" His response was quick and final, "I said No!" I went to appeal to my mother, "What did daddy say?" I advised her what my father had said, she just shrugged her shoulders and replied, "Well."

My father was increasingly dissatisfied with the situation that he created for himself. Yet, he failed to recognize that he was the root cause. He was not happy with his audio during church service, he was not happy with the way that the television program was edited. He would yell and scream at the staff during the week and embarrass the volunteers on Sunday. My father would stand in service on Sunday, unhappy with the way that his microphone sounded to him and call out everyone in the sound booth. He would mock them with a scowl on his face saying, "Come on we do this the same way every week and ya'll still can't get my microphone right." He would then turn to the people in the audience and say, "Turn and smile at your neighbor, show them your pearly whites while they try to get it right, I'm going to give ya'll two minutes to fix my sound and I am moving on." A grunt of displeasure would follow.

The person left in charge of Audio and Video after my husband's departure would cry real tears after most conversations with my father. He would depend on me to console them. My father overused one particular phrase whenever he was upset; a phrase packed with words that cut, and the words were especially hurtful to people who were giving their all and going above and beyond on a daily basis.

My father would say, "You are not doing what I need done, I don't trust you to make the right decisions." I was immune to the statement. I had been on the receiving end of those words many times before when I first started to take on more responsibility for the day to day functions of the church. I recognized that my father's intent was for the words to hurt. It was his way of shaking things up so that people would work harder to please him. For me, I had learned that the words could only have as much power as I allowed them to have. So, I started to respond with "Ok, let's talk about where I failed in this assignment that caused you to distrust me?" My father would reply "Well you know it's not that I don't trust you." Eventually he would stop using that statement in conversations with me.

Unfortunately, all the other staff members, did not know how to effectively handle my father's anger and harsh words. So I was the buffer, when my father caused staff members to cry, I would console them. My father would call me and say, "*So and so* is in their office crying, go talk to them." I provided the constructive feedback that he should have been able to provide so that the staff members would not continue to make the same mistakes that made my father angry.

I had a conversation with my father about the statement. I explained to him people do not hear anything after the word "trust." They are not comprehending that you just want them to make better decisions. People hear that you do not trust them personally, not that you don't trust their decision making skills and that is damaging. They want you to trust them, they are working hard to establish themselves to be someone that you can depend on. When you make statements like that it crushes them, literally. My father listened and for a while he made a change.

I was 25 years old, I was growingly increasingly more resentful about my daily job duties. I did not feel aggrieved about my parents, I was just increasingly annoyed about what I was asked to do and how I was expected to treat others. I wanted to leave but with my husband flexing his entrepreneurial skills, I considered my options to be limited. I threw myself into my work. Long days and nights. Things had to be done, the business was progressively moving forward. My work was what I was good at. I felt a sense of accomplishment when I completed large events or closed a big project. Ministry activities kept me busy. My responsibilities expanded daily. My father's vision was huge and I had to keep up.

The beginning of the fall season marked the annual conference where Pastors from all over the nation would come to see and hear my father's wisdom. I had simultaneous projects to deliver before the conference began. The largest of which was that the church was opening a restaurant, it needed to be ready for patrons before the conference.

One day while working in the building where the restaurant would be housed, a staff member brought me an offering bucket of change with offering envelopes that had been torn open. This staff member had found the bucket beneath a crawl space in another one of the buildings while pulling coaxial cable. I thanked him for bringing the bucket to me. I went back to my office, compared the money in the bucket to the envelopes. Someone had removed the cash from the envelopes and left the checks.

The checks were dated back as far as six months in the past. I called my father and advised him of the situation. His first response was "Fire him!" My father believed that the staff person who brought the bucket to me had removed the cash from the envelopes. I disagreed. However, this staff person was the same person who was a part of my husband's staff that had struggled with an addiction to crack. To my father, he was just a dope fiend. To me, it was just silly for the staff person to bring the bucket to me if he were the person who opened the envelopes. No one was that dumb.

My father and I had a heated debate over the next several minutes regarding who was responsible for removing the money from the envelopes. In the end, my father would win. "Fire him today!", "Ok Daddy, I will take care of it." That was probably one of the most difficult terminations that I ever had to carry out. In my heart, I knew that this man was innocent. However, my instructions were to let him go.

Over the next few weeks, we would continue to find offering buckets with change and torn offering envelopes hidden behind doors and in empty rooms. I went back to my father and said the staff person that brought this to our attention is no longer here so he was clearly not the culprit. "Can I rehire him?" My father's answer was "No."

I was at a loss, powerless to make the wrong that I had carried out at my father's request to this person right. Within the month, the staff person died a tragic death. I wrongly blamed myself, I convinced myself that he would be alive if I had fought a little harder for him. Things might have been different if he had not had to deal with the pressure of thinking that my father thought he was a thief. I was devastated. I should have done more.

The person who was emptying the cash from the envelopes was confirmed sometime later on surveillance tapes. My father never admitted that he was wrong in his hasty conclusion that the staff member was guilty.

My father continued to voice his displeasure on a daily basis about any and everything. He complained one day about the way that his office was cleaned at one of the church locations. We had recently contracted the work to clean the building to a couple with a cleaning business that were longtime members of the church.

The husband was a man who had served my father as a young man. Whatever my father wanted this man made it his business to get it for him. There was no task that my father could ask of him that he was not more than willing to do. I watched my father abuse the relationship. Instead of treating this young man with respect and honoring the servant in him, he disrespected and disregarded him.

My father wanted me to meet with the couple to voice his displeasure. The meeting was a complete catastrophe. The husband took immediate offense to the issues that I explained my father was having. He was right, there was no issue. The meeting ended with the husband storming out, slamming the door and leaving the building.

He later apologized to me but the damage that I created was already done. I had insulted him by suggesting that he was doing anything less than giving the special care and attention that my father deserved when he cleaned his office. But more than that, I had hurt him. The husband would pass away in his sleep a few months later.

Two people in a six month period who in my opinion died deaths of a broken heart. They were both too young to die; they were husband's and fathers. They were both a mother's son. They were committed to my father, committed to the church; both dealing with humiliation and thoughts of rejection.

My father would say that this is what happened when people were out of the will of God. People would actually joke, "Ooh I don't want to do anything to cross Pastor" implying that death would be imminent if you did. My father heard this and did not even attempt to correct people. God was not an evil God. The situation was insane to me. This was the place where I made my living but it was also destroying my life. For too long, I had not been true to myself. I would quiet my inner voice to please my father.

I heard someone say once, "She who trims herself to meet the demands of others will soon whittle away." I was quickly deteriorating.

Surprise

My husband and I were preparing to buy our first home. We had lived in a three bedroom house that my parents owned since the year after we were married. It was now six years later and at the time we had two children. We needed more space. It was important to me that we find a home that had room for the children to grow up but also had a space for a home office. I wanted to stay in a particular area of town and like most couples we had a price range.

We were taking our time to find the "right" house, there was no rush. Our realtor suggested that we start the mortgage application process during our search so that funding would not be an issue once we found the home that met our specifications. The mortgage process was more painstaking than the home search.

A few months into the home search process, I found out that I was four months pregnant. The time that we thought that we had to search for a home was quickly snatched away. A new arrival meant that we needed a larger house sooner than later.

Obtaining a mortgage was more of a lengthy process than we had originally anticipated. Each lender would return with the same response, We had too many open lines of credit and our debt to income ratio was too high. The lender's also mentioned one derogatory item on my husband's credit file, a department store credit card that had charged off.

Since my mother was a credit savvy person, I went to her and asked her to help me remove the department store charge off. It was an account showing opened before my husband was 18, he had no knowledge of the account so I did not believe that the account belonged to him.

My mother said, "It's probably an account that his parents opened in his name and did not pay, thats a shame." She gave me the language for a letter to send to the credit bureau's to have the charge off removed.

I understood the debt to income ratio reason because the lines of credit and credit cards that were tied to my social security number, used for the church were a contributing factor.

I knew that I had corporate credit cards in my name that were used by the church, I was aware of the credit lines that were opened by my parents when I was not yet of the age to consent to the contractual obligations of a credit card application. What I did not know was that there were so many of them. I took my credit report to my mother, asked her to look at all the credit card accounts. My mother looked at my credit report, kept it and said, "I will take care of it." I did not think any more of it.

After getting confirmation of the charge off being removed, the account was not his, nor was it his parents. I obtained an updated copy of mine and my husband's credit report and was shocked to see so many major credit cards issued by one particular bank. There were even more credit card accounts than on the previous report. I was amazed that one credit reporting agency listed that I had been in there system since 1987, I was thirteen. But, I knew that, what was shocking was that a different credit reporting agency credit report showed major credit card lines that were opened in 1980, I was six. Just in case, you did not catch that let me put it into perspective. I was born 1974, in 1980, I was 6 years old! I most likely barely knew how to write my name, certainly I was not aware of my social security number. Is it possible to complete a credit card application in crayon?

I never had considered the fact that my mother had obtained credit in my name to be questionable. As a teenager, I thought it was cool that I had credit cards with my name on it when my friend's either did not have a credit card or they were using their parents' credit cards. As an adult, I just thought the credit was necessary for the ongoing operation of the church business. At the moment that I was trying to get approved for a mortgage and credit that I had not applied for was standing in my way, I needed someone to help me to understand.

Family Business

May 2000, I was eight months pregnant and while working in one of the church's building, I fell down a flight of stairs when the heel of my shoe got caught in a ravel in the carpet. My doctor's recommendation was immediate bed rest until the baby was born which would be the first week of June.

The timing was awful, the Annual Women's Conference was less than a week away. I had no other options the safety and well being of my unborn child had to take precedence over ministry work. The Conference began without me, I trusted that the staff was capable of handling things in my absence. This was not their first rodeo and I was just a phone call away.

The Women's Conference would always end with a breakfast on Saturday. The conference breakfast attendee numbers had surpassed the confines of the largest banquet rooms available at any hotel in the city, so the ministry would hold the breakfast at the city's convention center.

On Thursday, the week of the women's conference, I received a phone call from my mother. She needed me. Something had not gone the way that she planned during the conference meetings and she did not want her breakfast ruined. My mother had a list of things that she feared would happen, they would run out of food, the set up wouldn't be right. Since I was the person who met with the event staff she wanted me there just in case.

My mother went on to say that she understood that I needed to be on bed rest but she thought I would be okay to leave the house for a few hours to oversee the breakfast. She was my mother, she had birthed children before, I was tired of being cooped up in the house anyway, so I agreed that I would come to the breakfast.

I arrived at the breakfast on Saturday, things appeared in order, the staff had everything taken care of. My mother still felt uneasy, so I stayed and made sure that she was always able to find me in the crowd. I figured that would help her to feel that any unresolved issues were on my radar and I would take care of it. There were no incidents, there was more than enough food.

Later that night, I started to have contractions. They would eventually stop and days later, June 6, 2000, our third son was born. He was healthy.

Six days after the birth, I received a call from my father, he needed me to come back to work. My father was not accustomed to managing the staff. The person who was supposed to handle my responsibilities while I was out had become ill and my father was trying to manage things on his own. My father went on to explain that the ministry's youth conference was to take place in two weeks. He did not think that the team working on the conference was prepared. My father said, "It's your sister's first conference, she needs your help."

As the conversation progressed, I advised my father that my baby was only 6 days old, he had not even had his second PKU shot, he had no immunizations and I could not legally leave him in the church's daycare without risk of losing the daycare's license. He and my mother had already considered that and had hired one of the teenager's in the church to stay in my office and babysit while I worked. This way my baby's interactions with others would be limited.

I told my father, that I would return to work the next Monday. He wanted me there the next day. "Okay,

Daddy I will be there." I hung up the phone thinking, how I am going to explain this to my husband.

My inability to say, "no" to my father was creating contention in my marriage. My husband was not happy about me returning to work so soon and he definitely did not agree with me taking our newborn out so soon. I convinced him that it was necessary. I think he just understood that he was fighting a losing battle as far as my family was concerned. My husband would spend the next four weeks driving me and our newborn son to and from the church offices for work. I continued to work with my newborn and a babysitter in my office through the summer months.

Tuesday, July 24, 2000, I received a phone call from my mother. The credit card company had called the church wanting to speak to the business accountant. The accountant had called my mother because he did not know how to answer the credit card companies questions. The credit card company informed my mother that they were calling about a refund check that had been issued on one of my personal credit cards that was used for ministry purchases. The refund was the result of a significant overpayment. Since the payment that created the refund was from a business account and credited to a personal credit card, the credit account had been sent to another department for review. My mother wanted to know if I had received the refund check and where it was. I told her I had and that I deposited it in my bank account. My mother wanted to know why, I really did not have an answer, I didn't really think about it, it was a check, it came to my house, it was made payable to me, I deposited it in the bank. My mother said we would discuss further when she and my father arrived back in town.

My parents returned from their out of town trip on Saturday. My father wanted my husband and I to meet him at their home. When we arrived my mother was reviewing all the bills from the credit card company for all the corporate and personal credit cards in my name. My father was disappointed that I had received the refund and deposited it in my bank account, but he was not angry.

I had not spent the money, it was still in the bank. My father wanted me to withdraw the refunded money on Monday and bring it to him when I came into the office. Since, I had not informed my parents about the refund check, my father felt that I needed to be dealt with so that I understood the situation was serious. He was concerned about me, citing that he had noticed a decline in my spirituality. My father wanted me to listen to one of his teachings on meditation and the importance of "feeding my spirit man."

He felt that I needed to take some time off but at the same time he needed me to be available for the upcoming single's conference. If I decided to take time off, my return would need to be earlier than the single's conference. He went on to explain that when I returned, I would no longer be on the church's payroll, my role and responsibilities would remain the same but I would be paid by one of my father's businesses and I would have a reduction in my salary. It would be a probationary period that no one needed to know about other than the four of us, my mother, my father, my husband and I. The period would last 12 months. One final thing, I needed to write a letter explaining my actions, just in case the credit card company pressed the issue further. My mother still owed a return phone call to the credit card company regarding the refund, she would call them on Monday and resolve the issue. That would be my Repentance and Restoration Plan.

Monday, July 31, 2000, I received a phone call from my mother, while at the pediatrician with one of my children. She had spoken to the credit card company, since my mother had not called back in almost a week, the representative that she spoke to had been reviewing all the charges on my personal credit cards issued by the credit card company and comparing all the open accounts, corporate and personal, where I was the primary cardholder. The representative questioned some of the charges on the corporate credit card accounts, he did not think that they were all business related. The representative had sent all the accounts where I was a primary cardholder to another department for review. The representative suggested that the terms of agreement had been violated by using the corporate card for non business related expenses. If the credit card company closed the accounts citing a violation of the terms of agreement, the church would lose all the open credit card accounts from the card issuer. My mother wanted me to know how to respond just in case I received any calls from the credit card company. I should confirm that I was aware of all the charges, advise that I was a board member for all the businesses, I should not agree that the charges were non business related, there was no way that the credit card company could prove otherwise.

My husband went to the bank, withdrew the refund amount and purchased a cashier's check to give to my father. Since I was still at the pediatrician's office and it was taking longer than expected, he met my younger sister at a gas station so that she could get the check to my father.

Tuesday, August 1, 2000, my mother called, she had spoken to the credit card company, we needed to discuss options to ensure that the credit card company did not close the credit accounts used by the church where I was the primary cardholder. I told my mother, I would do whatever she needed me to do. She was relieved, she had a letter that I needed to sign, she would be at my house in the next fifteen minutes. My mother arrived with the letter, it was a letter outlining all the account numbers with the credit card company where I was the primary cardholder. The letter was my consent to align all the billing addresses on the cards to the church address. I signed her letter and gave her the letter that my father had requested that I write when we met the previous Saturday.

Later that day, I received a call from my mother, the credit card company had not completed the review of the accounts. The accounts were all still under review. My father had some edits that he wanted me to make to the letter that I had written, my father explained the edits and the reason for the edits. The review at the credit card company had my parents unsettled, I could hear their emotion through the phone. They were scrambling for a way out. I told my father, I would make the edits and get a revised copy to him.

The next day, my mother called. She had spoken to the credit card company again. She was concerned about the time that the review of the accounts at the credit card company was taking. That morning when my mother spoke to the credit card company, they used the word "investigation." The use of the word was of concern to her and my father. The ministry could be negatively affected. My mother did not know what the "investigation" would entail. Above all, we had to protect the ministry.

The following Monday, August 6th, I received a call from my father's attorney. He began the conversation saying, "Kermeshea, you know I consider you to be a friend, tell me what happened?" My reply was "Nothing?" I was thinking to myself what is he talking about? What has he been led to believe?

He went on to say that he had some paperwork that he needed me to sign. "What kind of paperwork?" He explained that he had drafted a letter that I needed to sign, he clarified that the letter said that I authorized the charges on the credit cards without my parents consent or knowledge and a few other things. We scheduled an agreeable time to meet.

I hung up the phone and explained the conversation to my husband. He immediately said, "You are not signing that." I said, "Why its not that big of a deal, no one is tripping, it's what they need to get the credit card company to back off." My husband said, "If you never listen to me again in your life, you need to listen to me now. Your parents are setting you up to be left holding the bag on those credit card charges."

I decided that I would meet the attorney anyway, I went to the meeting alone. The letter was a document written for me by the attorney that just as my husband had predicted portrayed me to be an out of control spender who initiated and authorized charges on my own without anyone's knowledge. I advised the attorney that I was not going to sign and left the meeting.

The content of the letter was trivial, I did have the authority to make financial decisions for the church on my own. I rarely did. Furthermore, the payments were made by check from business accounts. All the business checks required two signatures and one of those signatures was usually my father's or my mother's. There was no such thing as only one person having knowledge of financial affairs. We had checks and balances in place. Even for accounts that the accounting team was not aware of, my parents were the check and balance. My parents could attempt to play the "I didn't know routine," but in the end documentation would prove otherwise.

I received a call from my father, he was on the verge of anger, yet pleading at the same time, the letter was an addendum to my Repentance and Restoration Plan, I needed to sign the document. I told my father the same thing that I told the attorney, "I was not going to sign the document." I went on to explain to him that my husband did not agree with me signing the document. My father inquired, "What does have to do with me?" My father and my husband had a conversation that ended with my husband saying, "I cannot let her make that mistake." I spoke with my father again explaining to him my position. I could hear my mother in the background saying, "Tell her that they have sent the file to the Fraud Department for review." My father ended the conversation advising me that if I intended to continue working for the church, I needed to sign the letter that the attorney had drafted.

Later that night, my mother-in-law received a call from my father. At the time, my mother-in-law was almost 60 years old. My father told my mother-in-law that he was calling because he needed her to speak to her son and encourage him to "do the right thing." My mother-in-law interpreted my father's call to be a threat and immediately called my husband. Knowing that my father had called and attempted to intimidate his mother, infuriated my husband and he called my father to let him know that. The conversation was not lengthy, the conversation was heated. My husband had officially transitioned from calm and collected to enraged and protective.

That night, I made the edits that my father had requested to the letter that I had written previously. I included my resignation in the letter. If I continued to agree to my father's demands there would be no end to the situation. I could handle the credit card company, the worse possible scenario from that situation would be that the credit card issuer determined that the terms of agreement were indeed violated and they would simply close the accounts.

If the accounts were closed, my parents credit was no longer in the shambles that it once was, they were credit worthy enough to apply for and receive credit cards for the church in their own names and could stop using mine.

My parents perception of the worse case scenario with the credit card company was drastically different. They feared being exposed. Exposure was potentially damaging; damage would lead to loss and loss would give way to failure.

The decision to give my resignation was not easy but at the same time it was not difficult. I was already miserable in my job, agreeing to my father's terms would only add to my misery. I struggled with the voice of my mind, the voice of my emotions, the voice of my family, the voice of the Holy Spirit.

I had always been an independent thinker. Spending so much time with my father, his confidence had shaped my confidence. My father's philosophy of keeping other's dependent on him so that they remained loyal did not apply to me and my husband. We were never looking for or expectant of a hand out from my parents. We had our own. I had seen first hand my father's ability to destroy lives, I was determined it was not going to happen to me.

I faxed my resignation to my parents home and called to advise my father that I had made my decision. He was more than angry, his response frightened me. He went on and on about how I was making the wrong decision. He said, "You really need to think about this.

Don't let that boy mess up your future." I explained to him that I had thought about it, my decision was final. I decided that I would use my talents to help my husband build his business. My father's response in the previous days had shown me that as hard as I had worked to make myself indispensable and valuable to him, I was not as important to him as he was to me.

The next morning, I received a call from my father he said, "Why are your kids still in my daycare?" I said, "Because that's where they go to school." He said, "You no longer work for me, your kids no longer are welcome in my school." I asked him if he was seriously putting his grandchildren out of the daycare. His response was, "I do not care about them, come get your children, now!"

Over the next several days, I would receive multiple letters, some from my father, some from his attorney, all with various demands. The letters were more threatening and accusatory. If I was not going to willingly bow to my father's demands, my parents had decided that they would place responsibility.

Moving On

When I refused to agree to my father's wishes and do exactly what he wanted me to do, it became an issue, a serious issue. I was not willing to protect my parents and the family business at the risk of losing my own family and not protecting my children. I had to make the best choice for me and my family. My mindset had changed, the choices that I made affected my three little boys, this was more than about finally taking a stand for myself, this was also about the downstream impact to my children.

My parents were using an attorney, so I sought the advice of an attorney as well. I knew all too well the unrelenting attack methods that my father would use to get the results that he wanted. I needed advice to prepare myself for the combat that lay ahead. I was advised that documentation of all interactions, the letters and phone calls was critical.

My father was the type of person that did not want others playing in his sandbox. To mask his own insecurities, he was narcissistic in his need to control others. I knew that by standing up and not being moved by his antics, I was setting myself up for more than a playground fight. People did not assert themselves when dealing with my father. They recognized the impending battle and would pack up their artillery and retreat.

Perhaps if my father had not attempted to strong arm me, the outcome of the situation might have been different. I was the product of 24 years of his training and preparation. I was strong willed, stubborn and a critical thinker. I was his child.

I spoke to my father several times over the next ten to twelve days, some conversations were civil, some were not. All the conversations were the same, my father would say, "I needed to make different decisions, I needed to open my eyes." I began recording the conversations with my father. He heard the beep of the recording device being set to start at the beginning of one of our conversations and became enraged. He had left me no alternatives, he was in all out attack mode, I was in a protective mode.

Within a few weeks, I heard that my older sister had started working at the church again, she and her husband decided to divorce. I had a conversation with my father in early fall, after speaking with him about my sister's divorce, he said, "Well you know what your options are." Without saying it my father was suggesting that I should divorce my husband if I wanted back into his grace. That was not an option for me, my husband not only had not done anything to me, but I had three sons, I would not selfishly take their father away as redemption for a relationship with my own father. I made my choice, I chose to stand with my husband. The time had long passed for me to leave my father and mother's house.

My father called me one last time, my mother had a letter she wanted to send me. He wanted me to know it was on the way. The letter arrived the next day along with everyone in my family's passports. My parents had the passport's in their possession since our most recent family vacation in early July. The letter was a page and a half long. The tone of the letter was defensive and derogatory.

My mother wrote that, the family met, my sisters agreed, I was legally disinherited, she was moving on. My mother spoke of my children, "I am sure you are wondering what about your children, my grandchildren. They are of no concern to me."

I was not surprised by my mother's letter. My mother had always been the type to become confrontational in letters when others could not immediately respond to her words. Furthermore, my nonexistence would allow her to rewrite the story of her existence, my mother could eradicate the mistake that she had made so many years ago.

My father called after I received the letter, he wanted to know if I wanted to discuss it. I was angry, I was hurt, my answer was "Not really."

Every day I was increasingly more depressed. My mother-in-law and my husband had to step up and care for my boys. I was lost without my father's input, direction, guidance. For months, I stayed in the house. My husband was still working to establish his business, our savings was depleting. None of my family members called, I felt like no one cared. I did not know what to do, I was lost; I had stood behind my father for so long, that I could not see where I was going.

I spoke to my father sporadically over the next few months. Twice the alarm system went off at the church in the middle of the night, I was still listed as the contact person. I called my father to advise him, he thanked me the first time, the second time he told me I was lying. The construction company that was set up to oversee the church building projects was being sued for non payment by one of the subcontractor's. I was listed as the owner of the construction company and I was served notice of the lawsuit at my home by a deputy. I called my father, he referred me to his attorney.

In December, my husband said to me, "It's been a while, you need to call your parents." He was right, but I was not going to make the call during the holiday season. I knew my parents, because of the timing they would perceive the call as me wanting something from them. I decided to wait until after the holidays had passed.

I called my parents home the second week of January, my mother answered the phone. I could hear that she was irritated to hear my voice, so I asked to speak to my father. He and I had always had the better relationship anyway. She placed me on hold, my father came on the line, "You are not going to call my house being rude to my wife. If you cannot speak to her like she deserves to be spoken to, don't call here." The conversation with my mother consisted of "Hello, how are you? Can I speak to daddy?" I was not rude, I was powerless to defend myself against my mother's accusations. I said, "I apologize, it wasn't my intent to be rude to her, please let her know that."

The conversation with my father was brief, it ended with us being nowhere closer to reconciliation than we were before I called. This whole thing had gone way too far. It seemed that I was the only person who realized that. I would have to learn to accept the things that I could not change while still praying that change would come.

Birthdays

Birthdays were always special in our house growing up. My mother always made sure that everyone's birthday was celebrated as if it were their own personal holiday. A birthday no matter what day or month was like an extra Christmas with my mom.

As an adult, my mother's birthday gifts to me were always a gift accompanied by a check. No matter where in the country my mother was, if she was traveling to minister or right down the street at home, she always made a point to make us all feel special on our birthdays.

On February 5, 2001, my 27th birthday, I was at home when the doorbell rang. It was the postal service delivering a box. It was my birthday so without even looking at the return address, I was excited. After signing for the package, I noticed that the return address was the church's address.

The box was taped closed pretty well so I needed scissors to open the box. My hands were shaking, it had been six months since I left church. It had been, a little less than a month since my last attempt to try to talk it over with my parents. I was thinking, they remembered my birthday, whatever was in the box was possibly an attempt to reconnect.

I opened the exterior box to find a burgundy velvet keepsake box. The box was beautiful, it had gold and silver stitching, ornate beads. I was convinced that my mother had remembered my birthday.

I opened the burgundy box to find mail, lots of mail. There were old bills, junk mail and bank statements, dating back as far as August. The mail was addressed to me and had been sent to my parents home or the rental house that we previously lived in.

❖

The next day, my father called. First, he wanted to know if I received the package from my mother. I confirmed that I had. That was all he wanted. "By the way, Happy Belated Birthday!"

February 1, 2002 I received an early birthday gift from my parents. The doorbell rang and there stood my regular postal carrier with a Certified Letter that I needed to sign for. The return address read:
Internal Revenue Service
Austin, TX

I opened the letter, I was being audited for the tax years 1997, 1998, 1999 and 2000. In 1997, I was almost 28 years old, I was not making a six figure salary in any of those years. I had never filed any exemptions or deductions on my tax return other than the standard deduction. I should not even have been on the IRS radar for audit.

I called the IRS agent listed on the letter. I was informed that the IRS had received information and a file from my parents indicating that I needed to be investigated for tax evasion. In addition, the IRS had received 1099-C's for the years 1997, 1998, 1999 and 2000 from the church reporting unreported income. I had thirty days to respond to the notice. My audit would begin in April.

I walked into the IRS Office the following April, alone, no attorney. The agent asked me a series of questions, all of which were focused on the church and my parents earnings. My response was always the same, "I am not here to discuss them." When she finally realized that she was not going to get the answers from me that she was looking for, she moved on.

The audit lasted for almost two years. The agent was pregnant and our file could not be transferred to another agent, so we had to wait for her return from maternity leave to close the audit. We never had to go to court. The investigation closed with my husband and I being cleared of all tax evasion accusations.

Death

The phone rang, on the other end was a friend of mine. She was the only staff person that had stayed in touch with me on a consistent basis in the six months since I had left the church. She remained in touch at the urging of my father who told her that I would need a friend for what he was about to put me through.

I answered the phone and she jokingly asked, "Where have you been all day?" My reply was "I am grown and I have children." We laughed and joked for a few minutes. She got really silent and said, "Maybe I shouldn't have started the conversation off joking, I have something serious to tell you." I think my heart skipped three beats and then started racing. I felt that lump in the back of my throat. "What is it?" She said, "Papa died and they wanted me to call and tell you." I felt weightless. In a near whisper fighting back tears I replied, "I need to call you back."

My grandfather had sent me a message through a family friend two days prior, he wanted me to call him. I never did. Now he was dead. To make matters worse, I had to receive the news of his death through someone outside of the family.

After I got myself together, I called the friend back. "How did it happen?" "When did this happen?" "Where is everyone now?" My grandfather had passed away earlier in the day, in his home. My family was there now.

I hung up with her and called my grandfather's house. My younger sister answered the phone. I said "Is Papa really dead?"

Her reply, "Uh, yes, who is this?"
"This is Kermeshea, why didn't anyone call me to tell me?"

"We don't need to call you to tell you nothing."
Click!

This heifer just hung up the phone in my face. So, I called back.

"Why did you just hang up in my face?"
"What do you want?"
"I want to know what's going on with Papa?"
"He's dead, didn't you hear me just tell you that"
"Bitch, let me talk to somebody that has some sense"
"This crazy girl just called me a bitch somebody better talk to her, blah, blah, blah"

My aunt is the next voice that I hear.

"Kermeshea, what's the problem?"
"I just want to know what's going on with Papa?"

My aunt went on to explain that my grandfather had passed away in his home earlier that morning, my cousin found him when she came home from school. No one had called me because they had been advised by my mother not to. It was my aunt who felt like I should know and had asked my friend to call so that she did not personally violate my mother's wishes.

I ended the call requesting that they just make sure that someone let me know when the funeral is.

Two days later, my mother called. The conversation was less than two minutes long. She wanted me to know when the wake and funeral would take place. She had arranged for a family car for me alone, if I wanted it. My sisters did not want me riding in the same car with them. I declined her offer and let her know that I would drive myself to the church.

About an hour after my mother called, my father called. He had a list of rules that he wanted to go over with me before the funeral. Really? Am I a toddler? Sadly, he was serious. The rules were as follows:

1. "Don't come to the funeral clowning, ain't nobody got time for your mess."
2. "Don't be late, the family will not be holding up walking in the church waiting on you to arrive."
3. "The repast will be at my church after the funeral, you are not invited."

I could not believe what I was hearing. Before my father could make it to number four, I stopped him. I told him that he failed to realize that Papa's death was so much bigger than the conflict between he and I. I am hanging up, "Goodbye Daddy."

The funeral was over without incident. I sat in the balcony of the church away from the family. I went to the graveside and returned home.

The next time I would be in a church in proximity to my parents would be in January 2007 at the funeral of a close family friend.

April 3, 2001. That day I mourned the loss of my Papa. I mourned the loss of my mother and my father. I mourned the loss of family. To deal with the pain, in my mind, I buried my family that day. In my heart they were very much alive.

Estranged

I live less than three miles from my parents home, I had been in the same home since two weeks before the birth of our third son. We live so close to one another, but we may as well have been world's apart.

In the month's that followed my grandfather's death, my parents had began making very public moves to erase my existence from their lives and from the memories of others. All of their books were rewritten and reprinted removing any reference to me. Their biographies were updated to reflect that they had three daughters and four grandchildren. The entire family including extended family were silenced to agree with the lies.

The "Hey Have You Heard" people would call regularly wanting to share the latest on my parents actions regarding me. I heard that my mother had all pictures of me and my children removed from her house; my mother had the locks changed on her home because she had a dream that I was standing over her in her sleep; my mother would lose her cool and blow a gasket any time anyone mentioned my name. My mother would boldly declare that she did not love me and was not going to waste a good prayer or God's time praying for me.

Members of the church who my husband and I had previously maintained relationships with would see us out or call, they would say, "well what happened, people are saying this, people are saying that." My response in the beginning was, 'people always want to act like they are in the know and speak on things that they have no clue about." My parents allowed the rumors to spread like wildfire and made no attempts to dispel them. I had done nothing but sacrifice myself for them and for the church on a daily basis. I made a choice that was long overdue, I stood up for Kermeshea.

I would eventually come to a place where I did not even entertain the rumors, when people came to me with rumors, my response was, "okay." The response was a subtle way of saying, "I am not interested." When subtle did not work, and people didn't catch the clue, I just said, "I do not want to hear it, I am not interested." I refused to defend myself against people's perceived truths. It was a lie and I learned a long time ago, to not waste energy defending a lie, my actions would speak for themselves. I could preach a better sermon with my life than I could with my lips. Additionally, I lacked the power and the platform that my father had to influence other people's thoughts.

In August 2001, after having spent a year at home during the day, I decided to go back to work. My husband's business was growing, but it was really a one man show, he had no true need for my assistance. I had one problem, I did not have a resume'. I never needed a resume' before in my life, so I did not even know where to begin to put one together. At first my resume' was a list of all my duties at the church, it was almost three pages long, it just looked unrealistic. I decided that I would focus on one area, I chose the human resource aspect of my job.

I began my search for a job, I interviewed well, made it to the final interview, past the job offer stage. I was the successful candidate for the job, provided that my employment references were successfully verified. I started to work contingent upon the confirmation of previous employment.

My new employer called the church, they would not verify my employment. I was at work when I received the call to come to HR. I walked into the HR Manager's office, he advised me of the situation. I could not believe my ears. When was this going to end, why couldn't my parents just let me live my life? The HR Manager looked at me and said, I know who you are, can you just bring me a copy of the last W2 from your job and I will consider that verification of prior employment. The next day, I brought him the documents and I kept my job.

I was still living my life disappointed, angry and hurt. At the time, I could not remember the last time that I was genuinely happy. I was merely existing. I was hurt by my immediate family's shunning of me. My older sister had not called, she did not reach out even once to see how I was, how her nephews were. I recalled all the times that she had needed my help after the family firings. I had never not taken her call, I never neglected to give her whatever she asked me for; cash, catching up car payments, anything she asked, nothing was ever to small or large for me to give. She was my sister and I always loved her and treated her like a sister should.

None of my family called. Not my younger sister who I had selflessly defended when she disappointed my parents. Not my aunts who I always loved and cherished even when my mother acted as if they were not her family. Deep down I knew not to expect their call, they all had so much more to lose by disobeying my father than to gain by speaking to me. They risked loss of cars, jobs and houses. All of that was far too much for me to ask that they give up, just for a relationship with me. I was on my own, my father and my mother had officially forgotten about me.

When my parents would hear that other people were talking to me, they would call the person and caution them against having a relationship with me. Specifically stating that I was toxic. It was as if they were determined to make sure that I was alone without a friend.

My marriage was suffering, my husband had stood by me and stood up for me in the moment that I needed him to. He loved me, he had proven it, by his actions he showed me, with his words he told me. I was angry with him but a different kind of anger. I now realize that in my mind, after losing my parents love, I did not feel deserving of my husband's love so I deliberately pushed him away.

In December 2002, right before the Christmas holiday, I walked into a nail shop. My mother was seated at one of the stations. I said, "Hello Mama." No response. I spoke again, still no response. I spoke to her calling her by the name everyone at church calls her since in her mind, she was no longer my mother. She said nothing, she picked up her cell phone, initiated an outgoing call and never acknowledged me. I left the nail shop without receiving any type of service, I was literally destroyed.

I viewed each encounter with my parents as if it could be my last. I thought what if I never see them again? I desperately wanted to just be able to be cordial and on speaking terms. I struggled with the manner in which my parents reacted to me in public places, on the phone and when speaking to other people.

Growing up, people would often comment on how I resembled my mother. We shared the same eyes, our noses were shaped alike. After that day in the nail shop, I was severely emotional. How could my mother look at me in my face, see herself, know that I was the child she birthed and turn her back?

I thought often of a conversation that my father and I had so many times before. Whenever he felt that I was not heeding his wisdom or in the wrong he would always give me a reality check. Regardless of if I wanted to hear it or not, I was forced to listen and make a change. When I felt that my father was wrong and communicated that to him, if it was a truth that he did not want to hear, he never listened. I would say, "Daddy, here is the issue, I have you as my authority. You are here to keep me in line whenever you think I am wrong. Who is your authority?" His response was always the same, "God is my authority." My response was, "See that's the problem, when I pray for God to speak to you, how do I know you are listening if I don't see a change." His response was, "You just have to hope that I listen."

I stopped going to church. I thought every pastor had secrets, just like my parents. I would sit in service and dissect every word of the sermon based on my experience in the church. I was wasting away spiritually. I prayed when I thought it was my last option and absolutely necessary. I wasn't mad at God, I was just damaged and hurt and that hurt was initiated by preachers in the church. In my ignorance, I didn't know how to separate God's love from man's actions.

In early 2005, I was watching a minister on television. He was teaching on family and God's ordained purpose for the family. It was not a message that I had not heard before. I thought, I need to call my dad, but I didn't. The next day, my mother-in-law called my husband, I could hear them talking, she was asking when was the last time I spoke to my parents. My husband said, "It's been a while mama." My mother-in-law said, "Okay, I just don't understand." My husband approached me a few days later and said, "I think you need to call your dad." So I called my dad. My mother answered the phone, I said, "Hello, Is daddy available?"

My mother replied, "Kermeshea, when you call someone's house, it's common courtesy to ask how they are doing." I thought to myself, here we go. I digress. "Hello, mama, How are you doing?" "I am fine, hold on." My father came to the phone, "He was extremely kind, he asked if I could give him a few hours and call him back." I agreed. I found out later he was entertaining company. The niceties were a front.

I called back later that night. I started the conversation, by saying, "It's been a while, I was just calling to say hello." My father began to ask interrogating questions, "What did I tell the people at the IRS?" He needed to know what they were looking for from him. So there it was, he was being civil to pump me for information. I told my father that I had not said anything to the IRS. I advised him of the questions that she asked me and told him my response. It was not difficult for me to remember my response, because when I met with the IRS agent my reply to her questions, was the same each time. "I am not here to discuss them." My father said I was lying and called me everything he could think of except for the name I was given at birth.

He went on to tell me how arrogant I was to think that I had anything to do with the success of the church ministry. He specifically said, "I never helped him with anything. I had no hand in any part of his ministry." The words stung, even though I knew that was his intent. I could not separate the emotion that the words triggered from knowing that his intention was for the words to hurt.

The conversation ended with me saying, "I am sorry that you are going through your issue with the IRS and I am sorry for any other hurt that you think I have caused you." It was so typical, he never realized the error of his own ways. He was fully responsible for whatever he was going through with the IRS. Did he really think that he could send a file on me and not create an inquiry on himself?

When I left the church, I gave my father a small booklet that contained the status of all of my open assignments. I heard that he split the document up between four people and that they worked my assignments

for years to come. For a moment, I allowed my thoughts to become selfish. What was he talking about? I considered all the church ventures that were my brainchild that were now closed, deteriorating or temporarily out of operation, in my opinion, because my father lacked the insight and passion to keep them going.

About a year later, I received three separate calls on Sunday morning from different people who had attended one of the worship services at the church. My parents had spoken of their recent experience in tax court. They were excited about a letter that they received from the IRS indicating that no fault was found. They went on to declare that a very close family member had deliberately attempted to destroy them by turning them into the IRS.

Of course, everyone who knew of our strained relationship and was within hearing range assumed it was me. I was too outdone, seriously, my father claimed to be from the ghetto, he claimed that he was a product of the streets. He should have known that a "snitch" does not have the option of not facing the person that they are accusing in the courtroom. If I were the offender, I would have been a part of his court proceedings, either by deposition or in person. The offender was sitting right there in the courtroom with him everyday, all he needed to do was pull out a mirror.

About six years after I left the church, I received a copy of a form letter that my parents would send out whenever people wrote in asking about me. The letter was signed by my mother. The letter was packed with the same defensive tone that my mother had written to me so many years earlier. The same words. Instead of my parents being an example of godliness and using the experience to positively affect other broken families, they used scripture to offer an excuse for their actions of hypocrisy and hatred.

The letter said, *"After a sufficient period of time of no repentance and no acceptance of the restoration plan ... [family member names] and I decided to sever all ties with them and we are at total peace with our decision. <u>As a family, we agreed to legally and naturally disinherit the entire Evans' family.</u>"*

I read the letter, there were two parts that stood out to me. First, there was the declaration of "total peace as a family." I had seen the other words before in the letter that I received from my mother in 2000, what I wondered was how my family was at peace? Second, the letter spoke of the choice to sever ties as a God approved choice. I knew that God would not violate man's will, that is why sin exist. I did not have a foundation of Biblical wisdom on God's approval for righteous choices. But, I was logical enough to know that God does not ordain a choice that is dependent upon a lie. He will not cause a person to lose credibility and taint their integrity because of a righteous choice.

The letter ended with the words, *"Also, there has been no attempt by the Evans to have a relationship with us either. We are all at peace!"* The text was bold and a couple points bigger than the rest of the text in the letter. I had reached out to my parents on numerous occasions since August 2000 only to be rejected. The statement was just another lie or perhaps it was my parents' perceived truth.

On top of all that, I had spoken to our insurance company some months earlier about life insurance policies that my husband and I owned. During the conversation, the representative advised me that there were additional policies on myself, my husband and my oldest son owned by my father. When I inquired if the policies were still active and if premiums were being paid, she advised that they were active and that there were recent payments. The policies were written a few years before my departure from the church.

The information just added to my anger and frustration. How is it that my parents did not want to recognize my life or my child's life, yet they wanted to benefit from our death? The letter said that they had legally and naturally disinherited my entire family, yet they were holding on to life insurance policies that would provide an inheritance upon our death. They were not holding on to the policies to pay for unexpected funeral expenses to bury us. My parents had often made it clear, in personal conversations, in conversations with others, through their lack of word or deed, they hated me. They would not be concerned in the least about insuring themselves for my proper burial.

I was always taught that when you make a righteous choice, you boldly stand by that choice, uphold the choice, there is never a need to lie or be deceptive about a righteous choice.

There are things in the natural realm that provided proof that I am my mother and my father's child. There is my birth certificate, my adoption papers, photos, my wedding video and the books that were previously published listing me as one of their daughters. There is the knowledge that members of the church who watched me grow up under my parents' care have that proves my existence.

Why would God validate something in the spiritual realm that could be invalidated in the natural realm? I was confused, I was tired of it all, I just wanted to be able to move on.

I regularly thought if I were still around my parents, I would give my father the public relations spin on his choice so that he did not appear to be a villain. My parents could have truthfully advised that they had four daughters, one of which is not a visible part of the family. After all the time that had passed, I still had a part of me that wanted to fix things for them.

In the months that followed after I read the form letter, I learned to accept that I could not personally change the nonexistent relationship between me, my parents, my sisters or my extended family. There is a saying, "If you are in a storm and you want peace, don't try to change the wind, change the sails."

For years, I had been trying to fix the situation on my own. My way was just exhausting energy. I had to reconsider my approach, change my direction. I tried to give it God and trust that His perfect will would come to pass.

In January 2007, the wife of a pastor that I was doing some contract work for passed away. This pastor had been a family friend for as long as I could remember. Through a series of events, my father and his relationship had become strained.

The church was small and had no staff members other than the Pastor, his wife and daughter. So he asked if I would help to manage things at the church on the day of the funeral. He needed my assistance in directing the efforts of his volunteer staff (ushers, greeters, choir). I agreed to help him out.

A few days, before the funeral the Pastor called me to say that he had a surprise for me and he hoped I was sitting down, my father would be delivering the eulogy at his wife's funeral. I was shocked, they had not spoken to each other in more than 10 years. I asked if my father knew that I would be there, the Pastor confirmed that my father did not know.

I went on to advise the pastor that I did not think it was a good idea for me be there. I did not want to be a distraction and if he was not going to tell my father, I could see nothing but harm coming from the situation.

The pastor gave his best effort to convince me that I should be there. His wife loved me and my children, she would want me there and my father needed to face reality. I still felt a little unsettled about it but I agreed that since I had committed to the Pastor that I would help him on the day of the funeral, I would honor my commitment.

The day of the funeral, my father, my mother, my sisters and their spouse's arrived at the church. It was clear from the look on their faces, the moment that they saw me that they did not know that I would be there.

I offered a "Good Morning" to my mother and my sisters as they entered the church. I received nothing in return, not even a small smile. I gave my father a program so that he knew the Order of the Service. He took the program and acted as if I was a stranger that he was meeting for the first time.

My sisters were seated in the pew directly behind me, my husband and my children the entire service and never attempted to make contact. My oldest child left the funeral wondering why his grandmother looked him in his face and did not acknowledge him.

My father fulfilled his obligation to minister at the funeral. After the ceremony was over, my father was so upset that I was attending the funeral that he did not show up at the graveside. Alternate arrangements had to be made at the cemetery to have another minister oversee the burial. I learned later that my father demanded that the pastor apologize to my sisters and my mother for my presence at <u>his</u> wife's funeral.

The ride home, I felt so defeated. In my mind, I thought that I was no longer emotionally attached to my family. To be in the same church with them for less than two hours was not supposed to have any effect on me. It was just one more instance of rejection from my family added to the many that I had come across over the last seven years. I thought that I was capable of seeing them as just another Pastor, his wife and his children. I was wrong.

Psalm 30 [2]

God, my God, I yelled for help and you put me together. God, you pulled me out of the grave, gave me another chance at life when I was down-and-out.

(The Message)

A Simple Prayer

"God Heal Me"

Three very simple words spoken in an almost whisper through tears that released me of years of pain, hurt, heartache and rejection. I prayed that prayer in a moment where those three words encompassed all that I needed. I believe that since God had been with me every step of my journey, even when I doubted His presence, in that moment, He knew exactly what I was asking for.

That day, after weeks of everyone in the house walking on pins and needles because of my attitude, my husband asked me a series of very direct questions, trying to get to the root of what exactly had me so on edge. They were questions beyond, "What is wrong with you?" He had been asking that for days and the answer was always a flippant, "Nothing." This day, his questions were different, they were questions that required a "yes" or "no" response. One of the questions was, "Is this about your family, do you miss them?" I immediately started to cry, not just tears falling down my face but tears to the point that I could hardly speak. After a few minutes, I was finally able to answer him, "I miss my daddy." My husband looked at me, through my tears I could see the concern in his face. He said, "That answer surprises me, and maybe I am not the best person for you to talk to about this but we are going to get you some help."

It had been a little more than seven years, since I worked at the church. Seven years since the demise of my relationship with my immediate and extended family. In all that time, I was still broken, angry, confused. I needed God to intervene. I missed my mother, my sisters but most of all my father. It is strange how women become dependent on and need acceptance from dominant male figures in their lives, even when the relationship is harmful.

On the outside, I looked like I had it all together. I could always smile and make others change their mind about what they thought I was going through or thinking. When people that I knew from the church or as a child would approach me in the grocery store or mall and ask that daunting question, "Have you spoken to your parents?". My response was always the same, "No I haven't and I am okay with that." My defense mechanism was in full bloom. Maybe that was just denial. I knew that the response would cause people to back off and not make me have to go down that emotional path.

Now understand, I was not emotional about not working at the church anymore. I really did not want to be there long before I left. I had given my resignation more than once and my father would tell me that I would never find a job that paid me as well and more importantly who was I to think that I could make it on my own without "piggy backing" on his faith. He would say, "You don't have a real college degree and you have no marketable job skills outside of this church." So, years earlier, when I landed a position where my annual salary exceeded the money that I was making at the church, it should be no surprise that the first thought that came to mind was that I had proven him wrong.

I was carrying hurt going back to long before that day in August. I thought about how my father had refused to allow my mother to give me money when I was still a child. How my mother had never come to my defense knowing that she had built her financial future by using me. I considered how long this situation had lingered without amicable resolution. I thought about how my parents who ministered to thousands of people and displayed compassion refused to transfer that compassion to their own child.

For years, at some point in the day everyday, I would say, "God help me to be a better mother to my children than my mother has been to me." I was praying the wrong way, I should not have been asking God to make me better than someone else. My prayer should have been based on my own personal needs without regard to my mother's actions. Like the saying goes, if you knew better you would do better.

So there I was, sitting in my 3300 square foot home, surrounded by beautiful furniture, two SUV's in the garage, healthy, intelligent children, a loving spouse that cared about our future together and I am crying over people that were not even slightly concerned about me or my children. How in the world did I get to this level of emotional instability? I had always been able to disconnect myself from whatever was going on around me and approach every situation with a stone face and logical thinking. One of my most admirable characteristics was my ability to be a pillar of unwavering strength even in the most dire circumstances.

I knew that a therapist was not going to be able to help me in the confines of 30 minute sessions. I needed a complete transformation. It had been a while since I had been in a church for Sunday morning worship, but the Biblical foundation of my youth was never too far gone that I could not tap into it. I needed the one and only Person that had never failed me to show up and fix me.

At the moment that the words "God Heal Me" escaped my lips, I immediately saw what appeared to be a movie of my past flash by in fast forward. I was calm. My soul was at peace. My tears dried up. The piece of my heart that had been shattered so long ago started to mend. I was instantly freed from the pain that had enslaved me. In that moment, I realized something that permanently altered my way of thinking and allowed me to break free of the hurt that was holding me.

People can only hurt you to the degree that you derive your self-worth from their opinions and need acceptance from them. I no longer needed my mother, father, sisters or members of the church to cosign my importance. God had already done that.

I started attending church again. I knew that my children needed the foundation of God's word in their youth. I could sit through a service and actually hear and receive the message. On the Sundays, that I did not make it to church I was grateful for webcasts and podcasts.

Things started to turn around in our life. We had been on a financial roller coaster for so long, even filing Chapter 13 bankruptcy. My husband's business picked up, I started to receive promotions and increase on my job. I renewed my faith in God, I was the only one in our house who needed to. Our future was brightening up. I began to realize that I did not have to subject myself to anyone's control for God's plan to be fulfilled in my life.

Forgive

To forgive is to cease to feel resentment against someone. Forgiveness can also be described as somewhat of a pardon or a release of liability for an offense. In the criminal justice system when a person is granted a pardon, their record is completely absolved, their reputation is completely exonerated. The person continues through life with complete forgiveness and the situation surrounding their initial conviction is erased from record and memory.

Human nature has a tendency to want to put the word "but" at the end of forgiveness. "I forgive you but I don't trust you" or "I forgive you but I haven't forgot."

Forgiveness is a process and it is a process that only God can help a person through. God is a forgiving God. The Bible says that God forgives our sin and "will remember the sin no more" (Jeremiah 31:34). God wipes the slate clean, "His mercies begin afresh every morning." (Lamentations 3:23). The Word of God is truth and its truth is not conditional to man's actions.

About a month after I had prayed to God to heal me, my husband was joking around and said, "What if your mom called today, would you talk to her?" My response was "Yea, but I won't be nice." When I said it, I knew I was wrong. I was immediately convicted. The heart has no secret that our words and actions will not reveal. I was no longer a slave to my past hurts but I was still ball and chain bound because I had not forgiven. It reminded me of when Jesus raised Lazarus from the dead. Although Lazarus was alive, he was still walking around wearing clothes from the grave.

I started to replay everything that I knew about forgiveness in my mind. I knew the Bible, I did not know exactly where the scripture was but I was reminded that, "if we do not forgive, neither will my Father in heaven forgive my trespasses." I knew that not forgiving blocked your prayers (Mark 11:25-26).

In my mind I could hear my father's teaching on forgiveness. "You can forgive someone but it does not mean that you have to trust them." I did not like the word "but" in that sentence. God's word on forgiveness was cut and dry, it was not conditional so who was I to think that I could add my own conditions to true forgiveness. To think about or say to someone I forgive you but I do not trust you still packs a punch of rejection. The statement itself shows that the offended person is still holding on to the offense.

My father had always taught me that when a person commits a wrong against me that I should forgive them, but I did not have to have any further dealings or communications with them because I was not obligated to trust them going forward. The issue with that is the offense or the wrong becomes the termination for all relationships. I know that all relationships will experience some type of offense, big or small, over the lifetime of the relationship. I was reminded of how my parents were never able to maintain relationships with their friends long-term. People were in and out of their lives. In my opinion, it was because my parents did not truly know how to forgive. I also struggled with linking forgiveness to trust, it leaves no room for restoration. God is a God that always provides a path for restoration. Think of the Prodigal Son. What about Judas? Even Peter, who denied Jesus.

My father would also say if he thought that someone was truly repentant that after forgiveness he would map out what they needed to do for him to allow them back in and restore trust. My father would provide the person with a written "Plan of Restoration" made up of his rules and barometers for progress.

To me that sounded like parole. I mean seriously all my father needed to do was ask for monthly probation officer fees along with weekly check-ins. My father's plans were not truly about restoration, they were grounded in manipulation which led to a person's humiliation.

Regardless of what I had been taught in church all of my life or heard from others, I needed to get forgiveness right for Kermeshea. Forgiveness was two fold for me. I needed to accept that I was forgiven. I was wrong for the way that I spoke to my sister that day that I called about my grandfather's death. I was mean to my husband. Though my actions when I worked for the church were based on directives for my boss, I still felt that I was responsible, I could have said, "I won't do that." I harbored anger and hostility towards my parents. I needed to acknowledge that my forgiveness was between me and God. My forgiveness was not contingent upon my mother and father's actions.

The second thing I needed to do was forgive. I had not made any progress on my attempts to restore my relationship with my family and it was not for lack of my effort. I had an expectation that my family would treat me the way that I had always treated them. When they did not, I needed to be able to forgive them.

All the times that I had reached out to my parents via telephone and been rejected. My sisters who chose to stand against me instead of standing in the gap for me like I would have done for them. My aunts and cousins who had silently stood in agreement with my parents decision to act as if I did not exist.

The relatives and others who knew that my parents were lying every time that they proclaimed that they had three daughters and four grandchildren and said nothing. The people who had spoken evil of me when they knew nothing about what they were speaking. I needed to forgive them and let it go so that I would be free to receive all that God had in store for me.

I asked God to show me how to forgive. I researched the word forgiveness, I found every scripture that I could on forgiveness. I read how God and Jesus responded to the repentant soul. I found my answer, I needed to pray. The Bible and prayer changed my thought process on forgiveness.

I had prayed and asked God to forgive me before. I did it everyday, it was somewhat of a habit. I would pray every night before I closed my eyes. "Thank you Lord for sweet rest, that Your angels watch over me as I sleep and that You renew my strength as the eagle. Thank You Lord that You keep a hedge of protection about us as we sleep, no evil shall befall us and no plague comes nigh our dwelling. Father if I have sinned today, I ask Your forgiveness, keep me in right standing with You. In Jesus' name, Amen."

I had prayed that prayer or some variation of it every night since I was a teenager. I knew that I only needed to ask God to be forgiven once and it was done. I had already prayed and asked God to forgive me for the part that I played in the situation with my family. This particular day I decided that I was going to do it again.

I sat down and I prayed.

"Lord, my heart is repentant, my mind is renewed in You. I want my thoughts to be like Your thoughts, I want my ways to be like Your ways. Please forgive me of my sins, forgive me of all that I have done wrong against my mother, my father, my sisters, my husband and Your people. Father, I release anger, frustration and confusion. I replace it with the compassion of Christ. The love of Jesus flows from my heart and I will love others with the love of Your son Jesus. Because I know that you have forgiven me, I choose to forgive. From this day forward, I let the situation go. People's actions, words and deeds no longer matter, I give it all to You. In Jesus' name, Amen."

The funny thing about not forgiving is that most people that you harbor unforgiveness towards never even know it. They are moving on and going forward with their lives while the person who cannot forgive carries the leftover baggage. I heard a minister not too long ago who compared unforgiveness and bitterness to drinking poison and expecting the person who offended you to die from it.

Over time, I gained a new understanding about forgiveness, trust and how they work together. Forgiveness is an action based on the past. Trust is confident expectation. Most people think of trust as a positive thing. I consider trust to be neither positive or negative. I can trust that a person will remain the same, negative and contrary. I can trust that a person is capable and reliable. Trust is a matter of choice and not conditional to man's actions. This is why I can continue to trust God when conditions are not favorable or do not appear to be in my best interest.

I think that a person's character is developed over time, character births integrity and integrity determines if people can trust you. Character is a sum of choices, ethics, traits and qualities. Integrity is just doing what you say you are going to do when you say you are going to do it. Trust is an expectation based on integrity.

A person can change their character by making different choices. The change in character will affect the person's integrity. The impact to integrity, either positive or negative will establish trust.

In hindsight, I think I was afraid to forgive. True forgiveness, opens a person up to an element of the unknown. Unforgiveness allows a person to make definitive decisions. Decisions like how you will handle the relationship and how you will control your emotions. Not forgiving allows you to bask in bitterness and consider unrealistic scenarios of how you will respond in close encounters with the person. Admittedly, I was scared. For so long, my defense mechanisms had allowed me to control my fears. If I forgave like God said to do, then I would have to always treat others in a manner that was pleasing to God. I could not bring up past hurts or situations and use them as a reason for negative responses. Forgiving meant that I had to really let it all go and completely relinquish the situation to God.

One of the things that my father taught me that I still apply to my life is to be principle driven. Principles are truths that serve as a foundation for my beliefs. The principle, precept and examples in the Bible are the blueprint for my life. I had read the scriptures and completed my research on forgiveness. The principle for forgiveness was "forgive and forget." My precept and example is Jesus.

I decided that I am a child of the Most High God, and God will let me know when someone does not have my best interest in their plan. So, why concern myself with other people's action. When forgiveness is necessary for me, whether I am the offender or the offended, I will pray for forgiveness and I will forgive like God instructs us to. Forgive and forget about it. I heard someone refer to forgiveness as "Contagious Hope." I am hopeful. I choose to put my trust in God. I trust that He will help me to deal with the frightening part. If I give Him what I have in the beginning, He will give me what I need to realize true forgiveness along the way. Trusting in Him will always yield positive results.

A few days ago, a friend of mine asked, "What if your mom desperately needed you, would you go?" Without hesitation, I said, "yes." She seemed surprised and said, "I don't understand, I know your story and your life has been turned upside down, why would you go?"

My response was simple, "I would because I am saved by the grace of God and I am striving everyday to please Him with my life." I went on to explain to her that the first commandment with promise is "Honor thy father and thy mother that thy days may be long upon the land....." (Exodus 20:12). The word honor simply means to have an inward esteem for their positions as my parents. I can honor my parents from a distance. In all the time that I had been away from the church, I had not ever wished or willed anything evil against my parents. I spoke truthfully about our relationship status because in my opinion, the truth can be told without malicious intent. When others would comment, I would say, "Just pray for them."

I love my mother, my father and my sisters. Loving them is a choice. It is an action based choice of acceptance, patience and kindness. I had to trust that God would work on their hearts in the same way that He had done for me.

My husband had told me for years, "Kermeshea stop living your life as a reaction to others." I finally got it. Regardless of my parents actions, my obligation is to trust God. People are flawed, if we were not flawed, God would not have needed to send Jesus.

Today, I am still a work in progress but the seed of faith that I planted towards complete forgiveness is blossoming into a beautiful flower. The most important thing for me is that out of turmoil, through healing and forgiveness, I have found His Perfect Peace because my trust is in Him.

The Bible says, "Blessed is the man that maketh the Lord his trust." (Psalm 40:4) A minister explained the meaning of the word "maketh" from the Hebrew translation as carrying the idea of not placing anything between you and God. He provided an example of going to the park and placing a blanket or towel on the ground before sitting down on the ground. A person would place the blanket between themselves and the ground because they do not trust the ground. I thought about his example, my children play football and I always carry a towel to the football stadium so that I can place a layer between myself and the stadium bench. It's because I do not trust what is on the bench. I thought about that rough financial period in our lives when I trusted my paycheck and my job and put them both between my trust in God to always provide.

When I learned to trust God, I accepted that there could not be a layer between my trust and Him. My parents, my sisters nor my extended family could stand between me and God. If you are wondering, how I am doing? I am blessed, I can say that with certainty because I made the choice to make the Lord my trust.

God's Plan

In the months that followed my healing and forgiveness, I often wondered, What do I do with all that God has given me? I am forever grateful for my life, every test, every trial, the good times, the not so good times. I am thankful for the time that I spent in church and working for the church. I am thankful for my parents, were it not for them, I would not have had the Biblical foundation to know enough to call on Jesus in my bedroom that day.

Working for the church, I gained invaluable skills that set me apart from others. Because of my experiences at the church, I can effectively handle multiple tasks at once, I respond to crisis better than most, I am a progressive logical-thinker. I am grateful for the opportunities that my life journey has afforded me.

Growing up, I was always reminded that my destiny was pre-ordained. God knew who I was and what I would be before I was formed in my mother's womb (Jeremiah 1:5). I believed that, I trusted that. My plans may have changed but God's will for my life had not changed. God made me with something in mind, never to change. I am not the workmanship of my mother's prom night mistake. I am not the workmanship of my father's manipulation. I am not the workmanship of either of their lies. I am "God's workmanship, created in Christ Jesus to do good works, which God prepared in advance for *me* to do." (Ephesians 2:10 New International Version)

I thought of three men in the Bible who derailed God's plan as a result of their choices. Some choices were necessary, some were not. The Bible's message about their choice and their destiny was consistent. God's assignment for them never changed, at the moment that they sought God and asked for forgiveness he rewrote the plan for their lives starting at the point of their repentance.

I thought of Moses. Moses was forced to flee the land that he grew up in after making a choice. He had witnessed a man beating up a Hebrew man, one of Moses' people. Moses became enraged at the injustice and made a choice to kill the offender. After spending 40 years in the desert, God called on Moses to deliver the Israelites from the hand of the Egyptians. God rewrote His plan for Moses' and used him to lead the children of Israel out of Egypt and into the Promise Land.

Then there was Samson. Samson was God's miracle to his parents. Samson's destiny was established before he was conceived. God chose Samson to deliver Israel from the hand of the Philistines. Samson's entire upbringing was dedicated preparation for fulfilling God's plan. Through a series of choices, Samson fell off the path for God's plan. Samson cried out to God and God redeemed Samson's life and rewrote His plan for Samson's life. God accomplished what He had established for Samson from his birth. Samson's final life chapter was that he delivered Israel from the oppression of the Philistines.

Lastly, I thought of David. David is often remembered as a true worshipper of God. David's end was the result of God rewriting a diverted plan. God had rewarded David's faithfulness early in his life and strategically aligned him to become King, a ruler over the land. David was a great King, he trusted in God, but David made some deliberate choices that altered the balance of God's plan for his life. David eventually called out to God with a repentant heart, and a renewed commitment to the ways of God. God rewrote His plan for David. God told David that his "Kingdom will stand forever." (I Chronicles 28:7) God's fulfilled promise was that Jesus Christ was born from David's lineage. How awesome is it that after all the turmoil that David's choices created, God still saw fit to attach the greatest gift of all to King David's legacy, Jesus Christ, the son of David.

I considered all the scriptures in the Bible that I had read about parents forsaking and forgetting their children. If the situation was important enough that it was addressed in the Bible more than once, I recognized that I was not alone, I was not the first and I certainly would not be the last. God's promise in scripture was consistent, "He would never leave me or forsake me." I was important enough to God that not only did he send Jesus to live and die for my redemption, God thought enough of me to stay around Himself, He was omnipresent in my life. He is the God of all comfort (2 Corinthians 1:3). Comfort is what I received from Him.

I came to realize that my assignment had not changed, the physical place where I would fulfill that assignment had changed. My life will always be a testament to God's faithfulness. God rewrote His plan for my life at the moment that I gave it all back to Him and made the choice to serve Him, trusting in Him only.

When we were Baptists, the deacons used to begin the service with devotion. They would sing "I love the Lord, He heard my cry." I have a renewed understanding of what that means. I love the Lord, He heard my cry. The Lord loves me and He answered my cry.

Whatever you are going through, I know that He will do the same for you. You do not need acceptance from any man to be in right standing with God and live out His plan for your life.

My Prayer For The Reader

Dear God,

I know for myself that You are a healer of a broken heart and You are the comforter for a wounded soul. My prayer is that you touch the lives of every person reading this book and where healing needs to take place, that the process for restoration in You begins today.

God I am confident that You can fix a dysfunctional family and that the power to reunite, restore and realize Your perfect order for the family is available and accessible to all of Your children. Father for those who are estranged from their families and reconciliation is not possible, I ask that You show them the path to embrace Your perfect plan for their lives and give them the courage to trust in Your promise that, "You will never leave them or forsake them."

Father God where forgiveness has not manifested, I pray that you touch the hearts and minds of all involved and show them that forgiveness is a gift from You that allows us to experience Your peace, to release anger and walk into overwhelming joy.

Thank you Father for the gift that You have given me...my life story. Thank You for being a forgiving God, thank You for Your grace, Your mercy, that covers Your children. For those who wronged their family members knowingly or unknowingly, I pray forgiveness on their behalf and that you show them the way to seek forgiveness on their own. Thank You for rewriting my life script when I deviated from Your plan and showing me how to get back on the path to Your promise. I ask that You do the same in the life of that person who needs that from You today.

You are an Awesome God, You are a Faithful God and I am grateful and changed to truly know that You call me Friend.

God, You know my hearts desire is that this book touches the life of every pastor, preacher, prophet and Bishop's child who has experienced hurt in life that they have not found the way to recover from. Show them Your way Lord, restore them to their rightful place in You. Heal their families.

I love you Lord and I know that their is no greater love that I could receive in return than the love that You have for me.

This is my prayer and I am confident that You will hear it and make it happen.

In Jesus' Name
Amen

Psalm 27 (The Message)

¹ Light, space, zest— that's God!
So, with him on my side I'm fearless,
afraid of no one and nothing.

2 When vandal hordes ride down
ready to eat me alive,
Those bullies and toughs
fall flat on their faces.

3 When besieged,
I'm calm as a baby.
When all hell breaks loose,
I'm collected and cool.

4 I'm asking God for one thing,
only one thing:
To live with him in his house
my whole life long.
I'll contemplate his beauty;
I'll study at his feet.

5 That's the only quiet, secure place
in a noisy world,
The perfect getaway,
far from the buzz of traffic.

6 God holds me head and shoulders
above all who try to pull me down.
I'm headed for his place to offer anthems
that will raise the roof!
Already I'm singing God-songs;
I'm making music to God.

❖

7-9 Listen, God, I'm calling at the top of my lungs:
"Be good to me! Answer me!"
When my heart whispered, "Seek God,"
my whole being replied,
"I'm seeking him!"
Don't hide from me now!

9-10 You've always been right there for me;
don't turn your back on me now.
Don't throw me out, don't abandon me;
you've always kept the door open.
My father and mother walked out and left me,
but God took me in.

11-12 Point me down your highway, God;
direct me along a well-lighted street;
show my enemies whose side you're on.
Don't throw me to the dogs,
those liars who are out to get me,
filling the air with their threats.

13-14 I'm sure now I'll see God's goodness
in the exuberant earth.
Stay with God!
Take heart. Don't quit.
I'll say it again:
Stay with God.

Let the word of God revive you. Let the Almighty God restore you. Let the Spirit of God refresh you.